TRUE TALES OF

*A Record of Personal Experiences
of the Supernatural*

BY
SIDNEY DICKINSON

With an Introduction By
R. H. STETSON
*Professor of Psychology
Oberlin College*

And a Prefatory Note By
G. O. TUBBY
*Assistant Secretary American
Society Psychical Research*

CONTENTS

	PAGE
PREFATORY NOTE	vii
INTRODUCTION	1
AUTHOR'S PREFACE	5

I

A MYSTERY OF TWO CONTINENTS	11
"A SPIRIT OF HEALTH"	25
THE MIRACLE OF THE FLOWERS	41
THE MIDNIGHT HORSEMAN	57

II

THE HAUNTED BUNGALOW

CHAPTER		PAGE
I.	THE CONDEMNED	75
II.	THE CRIME	83
III.	THE FLIGHT AND CAPTURE	96
IV.	THE EXPIATION	105
V.	THE HOUSE ON THE HILL	116
VI.	ON THE WINGS OF THE STORM	126
VII.	A GHOSTLY CO-TENANCY	141
VIII.	THE DEAD WALKS	152
IX.	THE GOBLINS OF THE KITCHEN	162
X.	A SPECTRAL BURGLARY	178
XI.	"REST, REST, PERTURBÉD SPIRIT!"	187
XII.	THE DEMONS OF THE DARK	200

PREFATORY NOTE

It is a pleasure to testify that the MS. of this volume of stories has been submitted with abundant testimonies from the individuals who knew their author and his facts at first hand, to the American Society for Psychical Research for approval or disapproval.

No more interesting or better attested phenomena of the kind have come to our attention, and we have asked that a copy of the MS. be filed permanently in the Society's archives for preservation from loss. These accounts by Mr. Dickinson bear internal evidence to their true psychic origin and to the trained observer scarcely need corroboration or other external support. They ring true. And they are, in addition, moving human documents, with a strong literary appeal.

GERTRUDE OGDEN TUBBY,
Asst. Sec., A. S. P. R.

April 5, 1920.

INTRODUCTION

THIS account of striking and peculiar events by Mr. Sidney Dickinson is but the fulfillment of an intention of the writer interrupted by sudden death. Mr. Dickinson had taken careful notes of the happenings described and, being a professional observer and writer, it was inevitable that he should preserve the narrative. He had been slow to prepare it for publication because of the prominent and enabling part played by his wife in the occurrences. After her death, when an increasing interest in the subject had developed, it seemed to Mr. Dickinson that the narrative might be received as he had written it—as a careful and exact account of most remarkable events. In reverence to the memory of his wife and out of respect to the friends concerned he could not present it otherwise to the public.

As the narrative is of some time ago and the principal witnesses are dead or inaccessible the account must stand for itself; the endorsement of the American Society for Physical Research

INTRODUCTION

testifies to its intrinsic interest. But the character and personality of the writer is a vital consideration. Mr. Sidney Dickinson was a professional journalist and lecturer. After graduation from Amherst in 1874 he served on the Springfield *Republican* and the San Francisco *Bulletin*. Later he was prominent as an art and dramatic critic on the staff of the Boston *Journal*. After extended study of art in European galleries he lectured before many colleges, universities and art associations. He spent some years in Australia, where many of the events of this account took place. While travelling in Europe and Australia he was correspondent for a number of papers and magazines, including *Scribner's Monthly*, the New York *Times*, the Boston *Journal*, and the Springfield *Republican*. During a visit to New Zealand he was engaged by the Colonial Government to give lectures on New Zealand in Australia and America.

His work and his associates testify to careful observation and sane judgment. Mr. Dickinson had an unusual memory, a keen sense of accuracy and he was cool and practical rather than emotional or excitable. No one who was much with him in the later days could doubt the entire sincerity of the man. There could

INTRODUCTION

have been no ulterior motive as the account itself will show. The narrative was written because he felt that it might well be a contribution of some scientific interest.

R. H. STETSON,
Professor of Psychology,
Oberlin College.

AUTHOR'S PREFACE

THESE stories are not "founded upon fact"; they *are* fact. If I may claim any merit for them it is this—they are absolutely and literally true. They seem to me to be unusual even among the mass of literature that has been written upon the subject they illustrate; if they possess any novelty at all it may be found in the fact that the phenomena they describe occurred, for the most part, without invitation, without reference to "conditions," favorable or otherwise, and without mediumistic intervention.

I have written these stories with no purpose to bolster up any theory or to strengthen or weaken any belief, and I must say frankly that, in my opinion, they neither prove nor disprove anything whatsoever. I am not a believer, any more than I am a sceptic, in regard to so-called "Spiritualism," and have consistently held to my non-committal attitude in this matter by refraining, all my life, from consulting a medium or attending a professional seance. In the scientific study of Psychology I have a layman's interest, but even that is curious rather

AUTHOR'S PREFACE

than expectant;—my experience, which I think this book will show to have been considerable, in the observation of occult phenomena has failed to afford me anything like a positive clue to their causes or meaning.

In fact, I have long ago arrived at the opinion that any one who devotes himself to the study of what, for want of a better word, we may call "supernatural" will inevitably and at last find himself landed in an *impasse*. The first steps in the pursuit are easy, and seductively promise final arrival at the goal—but in every case of which I, at least, have knowledge the course abruptly ends (sometimes sooner, sometimes later) against a wall so high as to be unscalable, not to be broken through, extending to infinity on either hand.

That disembodied spirits can at least make their existence known to us appears to me as a well-approved fact; that they are "forbid to tell the secrets of their prison-house" is my equally firm conviction. I am aware that such an opinion can be only personal, and that it is hopeless to attempt to commend it by satisfactory evidence; those who have had experiences similar to those which I have recorded (and their number is much greater than is generally supposed) will understand how this

AUTHOR'S PREFACE

opinion has been reached—to others it will be inconceivable, as based upon what seems to them impossible.

If what I have written should seem to throw any light, however faint, upon the problem of the Mystery of Existence in whose solution some of the profoundest intellects of the world are at present engaged, my labor will have been worth the while. I submit the results of this labor as a record, with a lively sense of the responsibility I assume by its publication.

TRUE TALES OF THE WEIRD

A MYSTERY OF TWO CONTINENTS

This story, as well as the one that immediately follows it, was first related to the late Wilkie Collins, the noted English novelist, with whom I had the good fortune to be acquainted—and who, as all his intimates know, and as those whose knowledge of him is derived from his romances may surmise, was an earnest and careful student of occult phenomena. I placed in his hands all the concurrent *data* which I could secure, and furnished the names of witnesses to the incidents—which names are now in possession of the publishers of this volume—equipped with which he carried out a thorough personal investigation. The result of this investigation he made known to me, one pleasant spring afternoon, in his study in London.

"During my life," he said, "I have made a considerable study of the supernatural, but the knowledge I have gained is not very definite. Take the matter of apparitions, for instance, to which the two interesting stories you have submitted to me relate:—I have come to regard these as subjective rather than objective phenomena, projections from an excited or stimulated brain, not actual existences. Why, I have seen thousands of ghosts myself! Many a night, after writing until two o'clock in the morning, and fortifying myself for my work with strong coffee, I have had to shoulder them aside as I went upstairs to bed. These apparent presences were nothing to me, since I knew perfectly well that their origin was nowhere else than in my overwrought nerves—and I have come to conclude that most cases of visions of this sort are to be explained by attributing them to a temporary or permanent disorganization of the brain of the percipient. Mind, I do not say *all* cases—there are many that are not to be set aside so readily. Again, it is not easy to arrive at the facts in any given case; even if the observer is honest, he may not have cultivated the habit of exact statement—moreover, stories are apt to grow by repetition, and a tendency to exaggerate is common to most of us. Now and then, however, I have come upon an account of supernatural visitation which seems an exception to the general run, and upsets my theories; and I must say that, having from time to time investigated at least fifteen hundred such instances, the two stories you have furnished me are of them all the best authenticated."

A MYSTERY OF TWO CONTINENTS

Some years ago, in the course of a tour of art study which took me through the principal countries of Europe, I found myself in Naples, having arrived there by a leisurely progress that began at Gibraltar, and had brought me by easy stages, and with many stops *en route*, through the Mediterranean. The time of year was late February, and the season, even for Southern Italy, was much advanced;—so, in visiting the Island of Capri (the exact date, I recollect, was February 22) I found this most charming spot in the Vesuvian Bay smiling and verdant, and was tempted by the brilliant sunshine and warm breezes to explore the hilly country which rose behind the port at which I had landed.

The fields upon the heights were green with grass, and spangled with delicate white flowers bearing a yellow centre, which, while smaller than our familiar American field-daisies, and held upon more slender stalks, reminded me of them. Having in mind certain friends in then bleak New England, whence I had strayed into this Land of Summer, I plucked a number of these blossoms and placed them between the leaves of my guide-book—Baedeker's "Southern Italy,"—intending to inclose them in letters which I then planned to write to these friends, contrasting the conditions attending their "Washington's Birthday" with those in which I fortunately found myself.

Returning to Naples, the many interests of that city put out of my head for the time the thought of letter-writing, and three days later I took the train for Rome, with my correspondence still in arrears. The first day of my stay in Rome was devoted to an excursion by carriage into the Campagna, and on the way back to the city I stopped to see that most interesting and touching of Roman monuments, the Tomb of Cecilia Metella. Every tourist knows and has visited that beautiful memorial—so I do not need to describe its massive walls, its roof (now fallen and leaving the sepulchre open to the sky) and the heavy turf which covers the earth of its interior. This green carpet of Nature, when I visited the tomb, was thickly strewn with fragrant violets, and of these, as of the daisylike flowers I had found in Capri, I collected several, and placed them in my guide-book—this time Baedeker's "Central Italy."

I mention these two books—the "Southern" and the "Central Italy"—because they have an important bearing on my story.

The next day, calling at my banker's, I saw

an announcement that letters posted before four o'clock that afternoon would be forwarded to catch the mail for New York by a specially fast steamer for Liverpool, and hastened back to my hotel with the purpose of preparing, and thus expediting, my much-delayed correspondence. The most important duty of the moment seemed to be the writing of a letter to my wife, then living in Boston, and to this I particularly addressed myself. I described my trip through the Mediterranean and my experience in Naples and Rome, and concluded my letter as follows:

"In Naples I found February to be like our New England May, and in Capri, which I visited on 'Washington's Birthday,' I found the heights of the island spangled over with delicate flowers, some of which I plucked, and enclose in this letter. And, speaking of flowers, I send you also some violets which I gathered yesterday at the Tomb of Cecelia Metella, outside of Rome—you know about this monument, or, if not, you can look up its history, and save me from transcribing a paragraph from the guide-book. I send you these flowers from Naples and Rome, respectively, in order that you may understand in what agreeable surroundings I find myself, as compared with the ice and snow and bitter cold which are probably your experience at this season."

Having finished the letter, I took from the guide-book on "Central Italy" which lay on the table before me, the violets from the Tomb of Cecilia Metella, enclosed them, with the sheets I had written, in an envelope, sealed and addressed it, and was about to affix the stamp, when it suddenly occurred to me that I had left out the flowers I had plucked at Capri. These, I then recalled, were still in the guide-book for "Southern Italy," which I had laid away in my portmanteau as of no further present use to me. Accordingly I unstrapped and unlocked the portmanteau, found the guide-book, took out the flowers from Capri which were still between its leaves, opened and destroyed the envelope already addressed, added the daisies to the violets, and put the whole into a new inclosure, which I again directed, stamped, and duly dropped into the mail-box at the bankers'.

I am insistent upon these details because they particularly impressed upon my mind the certainty that both varieties of flowers were inclosed in the letter to my wife. Subsequent events would have been strange enough if I had not placed the flowers in the letter at all—but the facts above stated assure me that there is no question that I did so, and make what followed more than ever inexplicable.

So much for the beginning of the affair—in Italy; now for its conclusion—in New England.

During my year abroad, my wife was living, as I have said, in Boston, occupying at the Winthrop House, on Bowdoin street—a hotel which has since, I believe, been taken down—a suite of rooms comprising parlor, bedroom and bath. With her was my daughter by a former marriage, whose mother had died at her birth, some seven years before. On the same floor of the hotel were apartments occupied by Mrs. Celia Thaxter, a woman whose name is well known in American literature, and with whom my wife sustained a very intimate friendship. I am indebted for the facts I am now setting down not only to my wife, who gave me an oral account of them on my return from Europe, four months later, but also to this lady who wrote out and preserved a record of them at the time of their occurrence, and sent me a copy of the same while I was still abroad.

About ten days after I had posted my letter, inclosing the flowers from Capri and Rome, my wife suddenly awoke in the middle of the night, and saw standing at the foot of her bed the form of the child's mother. The aspect of the apparition was so serene and gracious that, although greatly startled, she felt no alarm; moreover, it had once before appeared to her, as the reader will learn in the second story of this series, which, for reasons of my own, I have not arranged in chronological order. Then she heard, as if from a voice at a great distance, these words: "I have brought you some flowers from Sidney." At the next instant the figure vanished.

The visitation had been so brief that my wife, although she at once arose and lighted the gas, argued with herself that she had been dreaming, and after a few minutes extinguished the light and returned to bed, where she slept soundly until six o'clock the next morning. Always an early riser, she dressed at once and went from her bedroom, where the child was still sleeping, to her parlor. In the centre of the room was a table, covered with a green cloth, and as she entered and happened to glance at it she saw, to her surprise, a number of dried flowers scattered over it. A part of these she recognized as violets, but the rest were unfamiliar to her, although they resembled very small daisies.

The vision of the night before was at once forcibly recalled to her, and the words of the apparition, "I have brought you some flowers," seemed to have a meaning, though what it was she could not understand. After examining these strange blossoms for a time she returned to her chamber and awakened the child, whom she then took to see the flowers, and asked her if she knew anything about them.

"Why, no, mamma," the little girl replied; "I have never seen them before. I was reading my new book at the table last night until I went to bed, and if they were there I should have seen them."

So the flowers were gathered up and placed on the shelf above the fireplace, and during the morning were exhibited to Mrs. Thaxter, who came in for a chat, and who, like my wife, could make nothing of the matter.

At about four o'clock in the afternoon of that day the postman called at the hotel, bearing among his mail several letters for my wife, which were at once sent up to her. Among them was one that was postmarked "Rome" and addressed in my handwriting, and with this she sat down as the first to be read. It contained an account, among other things, of my experiences in Naples and Rome, and in due

[19]

course mentioned the enclosure of flowers from Capri and from the Tomb of Cecilia Metella. There were, however, no flowers whatever in the letter, although each sheet and the envelope were carefully examined; my wife even shook her skirts and made a search upon the carpet, thinking that the stated enclosure might have fallen out as the letter was opened. Nothing could be found—yet ten hours before the arrival of the letter, flowers exactly such as it described had been found on the centre-table!

Mrs. Thaxter was summoned, and the two ladies marvelled greatly. Among Mrs. Thaxter's friends in the city was a well-known botanist, and she at once suggested that the flowers be offered for his inspection. No time was lost in calling upon him, and the flowers were shown (without, however, the curious facts about them being mentioned), with the request that he state, if it were possible, whence they came. He examined them carefully and then said:

"As to the violets, it is difficult to say where they grew, since these flowers, wherever they may be found in the world (and they are of almost universal occurrence, through cultivation or otherwise) may everywhere be very much alike. Certain peculiarities in these specimens, however, coupled with the scent they still faintly retain and which is characteristic, incline me to the opinion that they came from some part of Southern Europe—perhaps France, but more likely Italy. As to the others, which, as you say, resemble small daisies, they must have come from some point about the Bay of Naples, as I am not aware of their occurrence elsewhere."

"A SPIRIT OF HEALTH"

"A SPIRIT OF HEALTH"

It is common, and, in the main, a well-founded objection to belief in so-called supernatural manifestations, that they seem in general to subserve no purpose of usefulness or help to us who are still upon this mortal plane, and thus are unworthy of intelligences such as both love and reason suggest our departed friends to be. The mummeries and too-frequent juggleries of dark-séances, and the inconclusive and usually vapid "communications" that are vouchsafed through professional mediums, have done much to confirm this opinion, and the possibility of apparitions, particularly, has been weakened, rather than strengthened, in the minds of intelligent persons by the machinery of cabinets and other appliances which seem to be necessary paraphernalia in "materializing" the spirits of the dead.

That the departed *ever* re-appear in such form as they presented during life I am not prepared to affirm, even in view of many experiences of a nature like that which I am about to relate. In the generality of such cases I am decidedly in agreement with the opinion of the late Wilkie Collins, as set forth in the preceding story—although I should be inclined to extend that opinion far enough to include the admission of the possibility that it was the actual Presence which so worked upon the mind of the percipient as to cause it to project from itself the phantom appearance. This may seem somewhat like a quibble to confirmed believers in apparitions, of whom there are many, and perhaps it is—while those who are impatient of ingenious psychological explanations may find in the following story a confirmation of the conviction which they hold, that the dead may appear in the form in which we knew them, bringing warning and aid to the living.

It is now thirty-one years ago that the wife of my youth, after less than a year of married life, was taken from me by death, leaving to me an infant daughter, in whom all the personal and mental traits of the mother gradually reproduced themselves in a remarkable degree. Some three years later I married again, and the child, who, during that period, had been in the care of her grandparents, at regular intervals, on either side of the house respectively, was taken into the newly-formed home.

A strong affection between the new mother

"A SPIRIT OF HEALTH"

and the little girl was established at once, and their relations soon became more like those of blood than of adoption. The latter, never having known her own mother, had no memory of associations that might have weakened the influence of the new wife, and the step-mother, as the years passed and she had no children, grew to regard the one who had come to her at her marriage as in very truth her own.

I often thought, when seeing those two together, so fond and devoted each to each, that if those we call dead still live and have knowledge of facts in the existence they have left behind, the mother of the child may have felt her natural yearnings satisfied in beholding their mutual affection, and even have found therein the medium to extend from her own sphere the influence of happiness which some may believe they see exercised in the events that this narrative, as well as others in the series, describes.

At the time in which these events occurred, I was traveling in Europe, and my wife and daughter were living in Boston, as stated in the story with which this book opens. In the adjoining town of Brookline there resided a lady of wealth and social prominence, Mrs. John

W. Candler, wife of a gentleman who had large railway interests in the South, and who was, moreover, Representative for his district in the Lower House of Congress. Mrs. Candler was a woman of rare beauty and possessed unusual intellectual gifts; she was also a close personal friend of Mrs. Thaxter, whom I have before mentioned and who introduced her to my wife—the acquaintance thus formed developing into an affectionate intimacy that ended only with Mrs. Candler's death, a dozen years ago. As her husband's business interests and legislative duties frequently compelled his absence from home, it was Mrs. Candler's delight to enliven her enforced solitudes by dispensing her large and unostentatious hospitality to her chosen friends—so that it often happened that Mrs. Thaxter, and my wife and child, were guests for considerable periods at her luxurious residence.

One afternoon in mid-winter, Mrs. Candler drove into the city to call upon my wife, and, finding her suffering from a somewhat obstinate cold, urged her, with her usual warmth and heartiness, to return home with her for a couple of days, for the sake of the superior comforts which her house could afford as compared with those of the hotel. My wife demurred to this, chiefly on the ground that, as the weather was very severe, she did not like to take the child with her, since, being rather delicate that winter although not actually ill, she dared not remove her, even temporarily, from the equable temperature of the hotel.

While the matter was being discussed another caller was announced in the person of Miss Mae Harris Anson, a young woman of some eighteen years, daughter of a wealthy family in Minneapolis, who was pursuing a course of study at the New England Conservatory of Music. Miss Anson was very fond of children, and possessed an unusual talent for entertaining them—and thus was a great favorite of my little daughter, who hailed her arrival with rapture. This fact furnished Mrs. Candler with an idea which she immediately advanced in the form of a suggestion that Miss Anson might be willing to care for the child during my wife's absence. To this proposal Miss Anson at once assented, saying, in her lively way, that, as her school was then in recess for a few days, she would like nothing better than to exchange her boarding-house for a hotel for a while, and in consideration thereof to act as nursemaid for such time as might be required of her. It was finally agreed, therefore, that Miss Anson should come to the hotel the next morning, prepared for a two or three days' stay;—this she did, and early in the afternoon Mrs. Candler arrived in her sleigh, and with my wife was driven to her home.

The afternoon and evening passed without incident, and my wife retired early to bed, being assigned to a room next to Mrs. Candler, and one that could be entered only through that lady's apartment. The next morning she arose rather late, and yielding to the arguments of her hostess, who insisted that she should not undergo the exertion of going down to breakfast, that repast was served in her room, and she partook of it while seated in an easy chair at a table before an open fire that blazed cheerily in the wide chimney-place. The meal finished and the table removed, she continued to sit for some time in her comfortable chair, being attired only in dressing-gown and slippers, considering whether she should go to bed again, as Mrs. Candler had recommended, or prepare herself to rejoin her friend, whom she could hear talking in the adjoining room with another member of the household.

The room in which she was sitting had a large window fronting upon the southeast, and the morning sun, shining from a cloudless sky, poured through it a flood of light that stretched nearly to her feet, and formed a golden track across the carpet. Her eyes wandered from one to another object in the luxurious apartment, and as they returned from one of these excursions to a regard of her more immediate surroundings, she was startled to perceive that some one was with her—one who, standing in the full light that came through the window, was silently observing her. Some subtle and unclassified sense informed her that the figure in the sunlight was not of mortal mold—it was indistinct in form and outline, and seemed to be a part of, rather than separate from, the radiance that surrounded it. It was the figure of a young and beautiful woman with golden hair and blue eyes, and from both face and eyes was carried the impression of a great anxiety; a robe of some filmy white material covered her form from neck to feet, and bare arms, extending from flowing sleeves, were stretched forth in a gesture of appeal.

My wife, stricken with a feeling in which awe dominated fear, lay back in her chair for some moments silently regarding the apparition, not knowing if she were awake or dreaming. A strange familiarity in the face troubled her, for she knew she had never seen it before—then understanding came to her, and the recollection of photographs, and of the features of her daughter by adoption, flashed upon her mind the instant conviction that she was gazing at the mother who died when the child was born.

"What is it?" she finally found strength to whisper. "Why do you come to me?"

The countenance of the apparition took on an expression of trouble more acute even than before.

"The child! The child!"—the cry came from the shadowy lips distinctly, yet as if uttered at a great distance. "Go back to town at once!"

"But why?" my wife inquired. "I do not understand what you mean."

The figure began to fade away, as if reabsorbed in the light that enveloped it, but the voice came again as before:—"Go to your room and look in your bureau drawer!"—and only the sunlight was to be seen in the spot where the phantom had stood.

For some moments my wife remained reclining in her chair, completely overcome by her strange vision; then she got upon her feet, and half ran, half staggered, into the next room where Mrs. Candler and her companion were still conversing.

"Why, my dear!" exclaimed Mrs. Candler, "what in the world is the matter? You are as pale as a ghost!"

"I think I have seen one," panted my wife. "Tell me, has anyone passed through here into my room?"

"Why, no," her friend replied; "how could anyone? We have both been sitting here ever since breakfast."

"Then it is true!" cried my wife. "Something terrible is happening in town! Please, please take me to my rooms at once!"—and she hurriedly related what she had seen.

Mrs. Candler endeavored to soothe her— she had been dreaming; all must be well with the child, otherwise Miss Anson would at once inform them;—moreover, rather than have her brave a ride to town in the bitter cold of the morning, she would send a servant after luncheon to inquire for news at the hotel. My wife was not convinced by these arguments but finally yielded to them; Mrs. Candler gave her the morning paper as a medium for quieting her mind, and she returned with it to her room and resumed her seat in the easy chair.

She had hardly begun her reading, however,

when the newspaper was snatched from her hand and thrown to the opposite side of the room, and as she started up in alarm she saw the apparition again standing in the sunlight, and again heard the voice—this time in a tone of imperious command—"Go to your rooms at once and look in your bureau drawer!" At the utterance of these words the apparition vanished, leaving my wife so overwhelmed with fear and amazement that for some time she was powerless to move—then reason and control of action returned to her, and she was able to regain her friend's room and acquaint her with the facts of this second visitation. This time Mrs. Candler made no attempt to oppose her earnest purpose to return to town, the horses and sleigh were ordered from the stables, my wife hurriedly dressed herself, and in half an hour both ladies were speeding toward Boston.

When they reached the entrance of the hotel, my wife, whose excitement had increased greatly during the drive, sprang from the sleigh and rushed upstairs, with Mrs. Candler close behind her, burst into the door of her rooms like a whirlwind, and discovered—the child absorbed in architectural pursuits with a set of building blocks in the middle of the sitting-room, and Miss Anson calmly reading a novel in a rocking chair by the window!

The picture thus presented was so serene and commonplace by comparison with what my wife's agitation had led her to expect, that Mrs. Candler at once burst out laughing; my wife's face also showed intense bewilderment—then, crying, "She said 'look in the bureau drawer!'" she hurried into the bedroom with Mrs. Candler at her heels.

The bureau, a conventional piece of bedroom furniture, stood at the head of the child's bed, and presented an entirely innocent appearance; nevertheless my wife went straight up to it, and, firmly grasping the handles, pulled out the topmost drawer. Instantly a mass of flame burst forth, accompanied by a cloud of acrid smoke that billowed to the ceiling, and the whole interior of the bureau seemed to be ablaze. Mrs. Candler, with great presence of mind, seized a pitcher of water and dashed it upon the fire, which action checked it for the moment, and Miss Anson flew into the hall, arousing the house with her cries. Mrs. Thaxter, who was at the moment coming to my wife's apartment from her own, hurried in and saw the blazing bureau and the two white-faced women before it and turned quickly to summon help—employes came running with an extinguisher, and in five minutes the danger was over.

When the excitement had subsided, an examination was made as to the cause of the conflagration, with the following result:

My wife, who was a skilful painter in oils, and devoted much of her time to this employment, was accustomed to keep her colors and brushes in the upper drawer of the bureau in her bedroom. She had also, and very carelessly, placed in a corner of the drawer a quantity of loose rags which had become thoroughly saturated with oil and turpentine from their use in cleaning her palette and brushes.

I am indebted for the above facts not only to Mrs. Thaxter and Mrs. Candler, both of whom I have frequently heard relate this story, but, particularly, to Miss Anson herself, who has been, at the time of writing this, for several years connected with the editorial staff of the Minneapolis *Journal*. In a letter which she sent me in response to my request that she should confirm my recollection, she set forth clearly the causes of the conflagration in the following words:

"Some time before she [my wife] had put a whole package of matches into a stewpan, in which she heated water, and set the pan in

"A SPIRIT OF HEALTH"

with these paints and rags. Then, one night, when in a hurry for some hot water, she had gone in, in the dark, and forgetting all about the matches, had dumped them upon the tubes of oil paints when she pulled out the pan.

"Every one of the heads of these matches had been burned off, evidently through spontaneous combustion. I went through them all, and not one had been ignited. The rags were burned and the whole inside of the drawer was charred. The fire could not have been kept under longer than the following night, and would probably have burned the child and me in bed, before anyone dreamed there was a fire."

THE MIRACLE OF THE FLOWERS

THE MIRACLE OF THE FLOWERS

AMONG the "phenomena" which attend the average spiritualistic séance a favorite one is the apparent production from space of quantities of flowers—to the supernatural source of which credence or doubt is given according to the degree of belief or scepticism inherent in the individual sitters. Having never attended one of these gatherings, I am not able to describe such an incident as occurs under such auspices; but the suggestion recalls to my mind two very remarkable events in which flowers were produced in a seemingly inexplicable manner, and without the assistance (if that be the right word) of mediumistic control. In one of these experiences I personally participated, and in both of them my wife was concerned—therefore I can vouch for their occurrence.

Some months after the happenings recorded in the two previous narratives, I was spending the summer following my return from Europe in Northampton, Massachusetts, at the residence of my father, having with me my wife and daughter. The mother of the child, who, as I have said, died in giving her birth, was a resident of the town at the time of our marriage, and her body reposed in our family's lot in the cemetery. The circumstance of this bereavement caused the warmest affections of my father and and mother to centre upon my daughter, she being then their only grandchild.

The little girl was passionately fond of flowers, and her indulgent grandfather, himself a zealous horticulturist and grower of choice fruits, had that summer allotted to her sole use a plot six feet square in his spacious gardens, which became the pride of her heart from the brilliant array of blooms which she had coaxed to grow in it. Her favorite flowers were pansies, with the seeds of which she had planted nearly one-half of the space at her disposal. They had germinated successfully and flourished amazingly, and at the time of which I write that part of the bed devoted to them was a solid mass of pansies of every conceivable variety.

At about four o'clock one afternoon my wife and I set out for a walk through the famous meadows that stretched away from the back of the grounds, and on our return, some two hours later, we saw at a distance the child standing upon the terrace awaiting us, clean and

THE MIRACLE OF THE FLOWERS

wholesome in a fresh white frock, and bearing a large bouquet of her favorite pansies in her hand. As we approached she ran to meet us and extended the pansies to my wife, saying:— "Mamma, see these lovely pansies! I have picked them for you from my pansy-bed."

My wife thanked the child and kissed her, and we went upstairs to our room together to prepare for supper that was then about to be served. A vase stood on the shelf at one side of the room, and in this, first partly filling it with water, I placed the bunch of pansies.

After supper I suggested to my wife that we should call upon some relatives who lived about a quarter of a mile away, and went with her to our room while she made her preparations for our excursion. While waiting for her I took from the shelf the vase containing the pansies, and we examined and commented upon them for some time; then, her toilette being completed, I restored the vase and flowers to their former position, and we left the room, and immediately thereafter the house, together.

We found our friends at home and spent a pleasant evening with them, leaving on our return at about ten o'clock. The night was warm and perfectly calm, and, as there was no

[43]

moon, the way was dark save where, here and there, a street lamp threw about its little circle of light. As we turned into the street which led to my father's house we passed under a row of maple trees whose heavy foliage made the darkness even more profound than we had known it elsewhere, and beside a high hedge which enclosed the spacious grounds of a mansion that stood at the corner of the two highways. This hedge extended for a distance of about fifty yards, and as many feet beyond the point where it terminated a lighted street lamp dimly illumined the pathway. We were at a point about midway of the hedge when my wife, who was the nearer to it, suddenly stopped and exclaimed: "Was it you that gave that pull at my shawl?" and readjusted the garment—a light fleecy affair—which I at once observed was half off her left shoulder.

"Why, no," I replied, "I did not touch your shawl. What do you mean?"

"I mean," she answered, "that I felt a hand seize my shawl and try to draw it away from me."

I pointed out the fact that I could not well have reached her shawl on the side on which it had been disarranged, and suggested that it might have caught upon a projecting twig; but

THE MIRACLE OF THE FLOWERS

although she accepted this explanation as reasonable she still insisted that she had the consciousness of some person having laid a hand upon her.

After a few moments we went on, and had left the hedge behind us and were within a few feet of the street lamp, when my wife stopped a second time, declaring that her shawl had been seized again. Sure enough, the garment was as before, lying half off her shoulder, and this time obviously not because of any projecting twig, since we were in a perfectly clear space, and could look about us over an area of several yards in every direction. This we did, puzzled but not alarmed at the twice-recurring incident; then, on a sudden, my wife seized my arm with a convulsive grip, and, raising her eyes until I thought she was looking at the light in the street lamp before us, whispered: "Heavens! Do you see *that?*"

I followed the direction of her gaze, but could see nothing, and told her so, in the same breath asking her what she meant.

"It is Minnie!" she gasped (thus uttering the name of my dead wife) "and she has her hands full of flowers! Oh, Minnie, Minnie, what are you doing?" and hid her face in her hands. I clasped her in my arms, thinking she was about to faint, and gazed fearfully above us in a vain effort to discern the declared apparition—and at the same moment I felt a shower of soft objects strike upon my upturned face and upon my straw hat, and saw against the light before me what seemed like blossoms floating downward to the ground.

As soon as I could quiet my wife's agitation and induce her to look again for the appearance which she believed she had beheld, but which she told me had now vanished, I made a search upon the sidewalk for the objects whose fall I had both felt and seen. They were plainly evident, even in the dim light, and I gathered up a number of them and carried them under the lamp for examination. They were pansies, freshly gathered, and with their leaves and stems damp, as if just taken from water. Hastening to the house, we went directly to our room, and lighting the gas looked eagerly toward the shelf where we had left the vase filled with pansies some three hours before. The vase was there, half-filled with water, but not a single flower was standing in it.

The next day was Sunday and all the family went to morning service at the church. As my wife and I, with our daughter between us and

THE MIRACLE OF THE FLOWERS

following my father and mother at some distance, reached the scene of our adventure on the previous night, we saw lying on the sidewalk a half-dozen pansies which we had evidently overlooked, owing to the dim light in which we had gathered up the others. At sight of them the little girl dropped my hand, to which she was clinging, and with a cry of surprise ran to pick them up.

"Why," she exclaimed, "how did these come here? They are the pansies I picked for mamma yesterday from my pansy bed!"

"Oh, no, dear," I said; "these are probably some other pansies; how can you tell they came from your bed?"

"Why," she replied, "I know every one of my pansies, and this one"—holding up a blossom that was of so deep and uniform a purple as to appear almost black—"I could tell anywhere, for there was no other in the bed like it."

So she collected all the scattered flowers and insisted on carrying them to church, and on returning home they were replaced, with their fellows, in the vase from which they had been so mysteriously transferred the night before.

It has been my purpose, in preparing these

stories for publication, not to permit myself to be led into any attempt to explain them, or even to embellish them with comment, and thus perhaps weaken what I desire to present as a plain statement of fact—yet this incident of the pansies seems to me (although for quite personal reasons) so touching, and so tender in its suggestions, that I cannot forbear a word or two concerning it. In thus indulging myself I am aware that the reader may think he finds a contradiction of the statement I have made in the preface of this book as to my non-committal attitude regarding Spiritualism. On this point I can only say that while I am not convinced as to the origin of the phenomenon, I should find much comfort if I could with assurance attribute it to a spiritualistic source. There are doubtless many who will thus refer it, and I write these lines in sympathy, even if somewhat doubtingly, with their point of view.

In every way this event stands unique in my experience—in place of its occurrence, and in all its circumstances. The town was the scene of my youthful wooing—the street one in which my *fiancée* and I had walked and talked a thousand times on the way between my home and hers. To this town, and to this familiar path, the new wife had come with me, and with us

THE MIRACLE OF THE FLOWERS

both the child of *her* love and sacrifice. Is there no significance, is there no consolation, not only to myself but to others who have been bereaved, in this episode? The loving gift of flowers to her new guardian by the innocent and unconscious child; the approval of the offering through its repetition, by the apparent spirit of the mother that bore her!—these things may mean nothing, yet in me whom they approached so nearly they have strengthened the hope that lives in every human heart, that the flame of our best and purest affections shall survive the seeming extinguishment of the grave.

Science, to be sure, has its explanation, and in fairness that explanation should be heard. To quote an eminent authority who has favored me with his views on the subject:—"The power that moved the pansies was a psychic force inherent in the human personality [of your wife] and exercised without the knowledge or co-operation of the objective self." (Dr. John D. Quackenbos.)

In other words, it was not the spirit of the dead wife that lifted the pansies and showered them upon us, but what we must call, for want of a better term, the living wife's "subliminal self." The vision that appeared and seemed to be casting the flowers was a freak of the psychical consciousness—there was no apparition save in my wife's overwrought imagination.

To quote again: "But that does not preclude the possibility of the levitation of the pansies, which levitation was accomplished by the lady herself, however ignorant of the operation of this psychic force she used objectively. The fact that she was thus objectively ignorant would be no obstacle to her subjective mind using in the objective earth-life her own supersensible attributes and powers."

The principal objection to this argument seems to me to lie in this:—the pansies did not first fall upon us, and thus, by suggestion or otherwise, so excite my wife's imagination that she thought she saw the apparition; the apparition was first manifest, and the rain of flowers followed. That is to say, an appearance of the immaterial was followed by a tangible manifestation—there was nothing imaginary about *that*. Had the conditions been reversed, the fall of the flowers might very well have excited apprehension of the vision—but I cannot see where there was any place for fancy in experience of this incident.

The second episode to which I have alluded

in the opening paragraph of this narrative occurred in the following winter, and was, in a certain sense, a sequel to the first. Business took me from my home in Boston, and during my absence my wife and daughter were invited by the lady I have already mentioned to spend a few days at her house in Brookline. Her husband was away on one of his frequent business trips, leaving with his wife her widowed sister, Mrs. Myra Hall, his daughter, a girl of eighteen, and a young German lady, Fräulein Botha, whose acquaintance the hostess had formed abroad, and who at the time was at the head of the Department of Instruction in Art at Wellesley College. All these were witnesses, with my wife, of the remarkable event which I am about to describe.

On the afternoon of the second day of my wife's visit, the child became suddenly ill, and as evening drew on exhibited rather alarming symptoms of fever. A physician was summoned who prescribed remedies, and directed that the patient should be put to bed at once. This was done, and at about ten o'clock my wife, accompanied by the ladies I have mentioned, went quietly upstairs to observe her condition before retiring for the night themselves. The upper floor was reached by a very broad staircase which branched near the top to give access to the chambers upon a wide hall, from every part of which one could look down over a railing upon the floor below—and the room in which the child lay was about half-way around this hall on the left-hand side.

The ladies entered the chamber and the hostess turned up the gas, showing the child peacefully slumbering and with forehead and hands moist with a wholesome perspiration, although her face was still somewhat flushed. As the night was a bitter cold one in mid-January, the mistress of the house suggested that some additional covering should be placed upon the bed, and produced from another room an eider-down counterpane, covered with scarlet silk, which was carefully arranged without waking the sleeper. All then left the room and started downstairs again, the hostess being the last to go out, after lowering the gas until it showed only a point of light.

They were near the bottom of the staircase when my wife suddenly cried out: "Oh, there is Minnie! She passed up the stairs by me, all in white, and has gone into the room! Oh, I know something dreadful is going to happen!"—and she rushed frantically to the upper floor, followed by the others in a body. At the half-open door of the child's room they all stopped and listened, not daring for the moment to enter, but no sound came from within. Then, mustering up courage and clinging to each others' hands, they went softly in, and the hostess turned up the gas. With one accord they looked toward the bed, and, half-blinded by the sudden glare of the gaslight, could not for a moment credit what their eyes showed them—that the sleeping child was lying under a coverlet, not of scarlet, as they had left her hardly a minute before, but of snowy white. Recovering from their astonishment, an examination revealed the cause of the phenomenon. The scarlet eider-down counterpane was in its place, but completely covered with pure white lilies on long stalks, so spread about and lying in such quantities that the surface of the bed was hidden under their blooms. By actual count there were more than two hundred of these rich and beautiful blossoms strewn upon the coverlet, representing a moderate fortune at that time of year, and probably unprocurable though all the conservatories in the city had been searched for them.

They were carefully gathered and placed about the house in vases, jugs, and every other receptacle that could be pressed into service to hold them, filling the rooms for several days with their fragrance until, like other flowers, they faded and died.

THE MIDNIGHT HORSEMAN

THE MIDNIGHT HORSEMAN

On a brilliant moonlit evening in August, 1885, a considerable party of friends and more or less intimate acquaintances of the hostess assembled at the summer cottage of Mrs. Thaxter at Appledore Island, Isles of Shoals. Included in the company were the then editor of the New York *Herald*, Rev. Dr. Hepworth, —also well known as a prominent divine and pulpit orator—two of the leading musicians of Boston (Julius Eichberg and Prof. John K. Paine)—of whom one occupied a chair in Harvard University,—and, among others, my wife and myself. The cottage was the charming resort which the visitor would be led to expect from the well-known refinement and artistic taste of its occupant, and its interior attractions might well have been suggested even to the casual passer-by who looked upon its wonderful flower-garden, wherein seeds of every variety had in spring been scattered broadcast and in profusion, and now, as autumn approached, had developed into a jungle of blooms of every conceivable color.

We had some music, as I remember, and after that an interesting conversation, which, in consequence of the many varied and brilliant intellects there assembled, took a wide range, coming around finally—I do not recall by what steps—to occultism, clairvoyance, and the phenomena of so-called "Spiritualism." In the course of the discussion of this topic, the editor interested us by a humorous account of some recent experiences of his own in "table-tipping" and "communications" by rappings—and incidentally remarked that he believed any assembly of persons who wished could experience similar phenomena, even though none of them possessed what it is usual to describe as "mediumistic" powers. Some one else then suggested that, as our company seemed to fulfil this condition, the present might be a favorable time to test the theory—whereupon we all proceeded to the adjoining dining-room with the view of making experiment by means of the large dinner table that stood in the middle of it.

(I may here state that although my wife had already had some abnormal experiences, only Mrs. Thaxter and I were acquainted with the fact, and even these had come to her unsought in every instance.)

Somewhat to our disappointment, the table failed to show itself susceptible to any "influence" other than the law of gravitation, but remained insensible and immovable, even though we sat about it under approved "conditions" for half an hour or so—lights lowered, and our imposed hands touching each other in order to form upon it an uninterrupted "circuit." We finally tired of this dull sport, turned up the lights, and pushing back our chairs from the table, fell into general conversation.

Hardly had we done so, when my wife suddenly exclaimed:—"How strange! Why, the wall of the room seems to have been removed, and I can see rocks and the sea, and the moonlight shining upon them!" At this interruption our talk naturally ceased abruptly, and one of us asked her to describe more in detail what was visible to her.

"It is growing stranger still," she replied. "I do not see the sea any more. I see a long, straight road, with great trees like elms here and there on the side of it, and casting dark shadows across it. There are no trees like those and no such road near here, and I cannot understand it. There is a man standing in the middle of the road, in the shadow of one of the trees. Now he is coming toward me and I can see his face in the moonlight. Why! it is John Weiss!" (naming the Liberal clergyman and writer whom most of us had known in Boston, and who had died some five or six years before) "Why, is that you? What are you doing here, and what does this mean? He smiles, but does not speak. Now he has turned and gone back into the shadow of the tree again."

After a few moments' pause:—"Now I can see something coming along the road some distance away. It is a man on horseback. He is riding slowly, and he has his head bent and a slouch hat over his eyes, so that I cannot see his face. Now John Weiss steps out of the shadow into the moonlight; the horse sees him and stops—he rears up in the air and whirls about and begins to run back in the direction from which he came. The man on his back pulls him up, lashes him with his whip, turns him around, and tries to make him go forward. The horse is terrified and backs again, trying to break away from his rider; the man strikes him again, but he will not advance.

"The man dismounts and tries to lead the horse, looking about to see what he is frightened at. I can see his face now very clearly— I should know him anywhere! John Weiss is walking toward him, but the man does not see him. The horse does, though, and plunges and struggles, but the man in strong and holds him fast. Now John Weiss is so close to the man that he *must* see him. Oh! Oh! he does see him, and is horribly frightened! He steps back but John Weiss does not follow—only points his hand at him. The man jumps on his horse and beats him fiercely with his whip, and the two fly back down the road and disappear in the distance. Tell me, John Weiss, what it all means? He smiles again and shakes his head—now *he* is gone, too; I can see nothing more."

We were all profoundly impressed by this graphic recital and spent some time discussing what possible meaning the strange vision could have; but we were compelled to abandon all efforts to elucidate it, and it was not until some seven months later that the sequel to the mystery was furnished—a sequel that for the moment seemed about to offer an explanation, but, if anything, beclouded the matter even more deeply than before.

Early in March of the following year a party of eight or ten persons was dining at the house of Mrs. Candler, in Brookline, already mentioned in this series, and after dinner went up to the sitting-room of the hostess, upon the second floor. The weather for a week previous had been warm and spring-like, but on the day in question a heavy snowstorm had been raging, which cleared at nightfall, leaving a foot or so of snow upon the ground. Of the dinner-party only my wife and I had been at the Isles of Shoals the previous summer when the incident above narrated had occurred;—but all present were acquainted with the circumstance, which had been a frequent subject of conversation among us at our frequent gatherings at one another's houses during the autumn and winter that had followed.

As I sat near the door and let my eye wander about the apartment, I idly noticed, among the many souvenirs of foreign travel which it contained, two Japanese vases set upon brackets in opposite corners, and about six feet from the floor. These vases were, perhaps, twenty feet apart—the width of the room. The vase on the bracket at my right was empty, while the other contained a bunch of "pussy-willows," which attracted my attention as the usual season for these growths had not arrived. I commented upon this circumstance to my hostess, who replied:—"Yes, it is very early for them, is it not? I was driving yesterday, and was surprised to see a willow-tree bearing those 'pussies' in a sheltered spot beside Jamaica Pond. I had the footman get down and gather them, and when I reached home I put them in that vase."

This remark, of course, drew all eyes to the bracket bearing the vase filled with the "pussies" —which, thereupon and at the instant, disappeared, leaving the vase in its place, but quite empty; a soft thud was heard as two or three of the stalks fell upon the carpet midway between the two brackets, and a rustling sound in the right-hand corner attracted the attention of all present to the singular fact that the "pussies" were now standing in the vase on the second bracket as quietly as if they had been there at the outset.

It is to be noted that no one in the room was within a dozen feet of either of the two vases, and that neither of them could be reached by anyone who did not stand upon a chair for the purpose. Moreover, the room was brilliantly illuminated by several gas-jets. We had been accustomed to singular happenings in this particular house, and consequently were amused rather than startled by the whimsical nature of this one. In discussing it some one suggested that peculiar influences seemed to be about, and it was agreed to invite them to further manifestations if possible. Consequently the centre of the room was cleared and a large table moved into it—around which, after locking the door that led into the hall, and extinguishing all the lights but one (which also was turned down to a faint glimmer), we drew up our chairs and awaited developments. A half-hour passed without anything whatever happening—whereupon, deciding that conditions were unfavorable, we relighted all the gas-jets and fell into general conversation, although leaving the table still in its position in the middle of the room.

In a few minutes our hostess said:—"Oh, by the way, I want you to see the new decorations I have had placed in my daughter's room. You know it is her birthday"—in fact, I believe that evening's dinner party was in honor of the event—"and I have had her room entirely refitted, since she is no longer a girl, but a young lady."

So, following her lead, we all trooped away to inspect the new arrangement. In doing so we passed down the hall for a distance of some fifty feet, and entered the room in question, which was at the front of the house and overlooked its extensive grounds. The apartment was decorated with all the luxury and display of taste that large means and the command of expert skill could provide, and we spent some time in examination of its rich and beautiful details.

One item that particularly attracted our attention was a small but very heavy clock that stood on the mantelpiece, its case of Japanese carved bronze, and its interior mechanism giving forth a very peculiarly musical and rapid "tick-tock, tick-tock" as its short pendulum swung to and fro. It was, in fact, a unique and curious ornament, and all the members of the party admiringly examined it—for my own part, I was so struck with its rare character that I stood regarding it after the others had left the room, and turned from it only when our hostess, who alone remained, playfully inquired if I intended to study the clock all night, and, extinguishing the light, passed out into the hall with me.

Returning to the sitting-room, we decided to make some further experiment, and, again extinguishing the lights and relocking the door leading into the hall, seated ourselves around the table as before. We had not been in this position more than a few minutes when there came a tremendous thump upon the table, like the fall of some heavy object. Being nearest to the lowered gas-jet which gave the only light to the room, I jumped up and turned it on to its full capacity—whereupon everyone present saw standing, in the exact centre of the table, its "tick-tock, tick-tock" ringing out sonorously, the carved bronze clock which we had so recently inspected in the distant bedchamber, and which had been passed in some mysterious fashion along fifty feet of hall space, and through a shut and locked door, to astonish us by its present appearance.

Forming ourselves into a committee of the whole, we carried the clock back to its former place, which, it need not be said, we found unoccupied—then returned to the sitting-room, where, with lowered lights, we discussed the strange occurrences of the evening. Although curious to see if any other manifestations would occur, we made no effort to invite them beyond dimming the lights, and as we found the room had become rather warm and close, we opened the door into the hall for the sake of better ventilation. The hall was only partially lighted, but objects in it were easily visible in comparison with the almost total darkness that shrouded the sitting-room. Our talk was of ghosts and of other subjects uncanny to the uninitiated, and might have seemed unpleasantly interesting to anyone listening to it from the hall—as we were afterward led to believe was the case.

Directly facing the open door, and the only one of the company so seated, was my wife—who suddenly startled us all by springing to her feet and crying out:—"There he is! There is the man I saw at the Isles of Shoals last summer!"

"What is it?" we inquired; "an apparition?"

"No, no!" she exclaimed; "it is a living man! I saw him look around the edge of the door and immediately draw back again! He is here to rob the house! Stop him! Stop him!"—and she rushed out into the hall with the whole company in pursuit. The servants, who by this time had gone to bed, were aroused and set to work to examine the lower floors, while we above searched every room, but in each case without result.

Next to the sitting-room was a large apartment some thirty feet long by twenty wide, which was used for dancing parties, and dinners on occasions when many guests were invited. It was at the time unfurnished, except, I believe, that a few chairs were scattered about it, and along one side was a row of several windows, before which hung heavy crimson draperies that completely covered them. We lighted the gas in this room, but a glance was sufficient to show that it was unoccupied and afforded no possible place of concealment. I passed through it, however, and, as I did so, felt a current of cold air, which I immediately traced, by the swaying of one of the heavy curtains, to a window which its folds covered.

Going up to the drapery and drawing it aside, I saw that the window behind it was half open, and on the sill and the stone coping outside I perceived, in the several inches of snow that covered both, marks which showed the passage of what was evidently a human body. Reaching nearly to the window was the slanting roof, formed by heavy plate glass, of the conservatory, which opened from the dining-room on the lower floor—and in the snow which covered this was a furrow which indicated that someone had by this means allowed himself to slide from the second story to the ground. Further investigation below showed, by the tell-tale marks in the snow, that the person who had thus escaped from the house, and who, after gliding down the glass roof of the conservatory, had fallen sprawling under it, had lost no time in picking himself up, and making good his escape. The footsteps of a man running with long strides were traced through the grounds to the street, two hundred yards away, where they were lost in the confused tracks of the public highway—and from that time to the present the mystery has remained unsolved.

THE HAUNTED BUNGALOW

THE HAUNTED BUNGALOW

Prefatory Note

The annals of crime contain few chapters more lurid than those contributed to them by the record of Frederick Bailey Deeming, who suffered the extreme penalty of the law on the scaffold of the Melbourne (Victoria, Australia) jail on the morning of the twenty-third of May, in the year one thousasnd, eight hundred and ninety-two.

The details of his misdeeds, his trial, and his punishment were set forth by me at the time in letters to the New York *Times* and the Boston *Journal*—of which, as well as of several other publications, I was accredited correspondent during several years of residence and travel in Australasia and the South Seas.

In the narrative that follows, so far as it describes atrocities which shocked the whole English-speaking world, I have endeavored to subordinate particulars in the presentation of a general effect; my purpose has been, not to picture horrors, but to suggest the strange and abnormal personality that lay behind them.

In regard to the peculiar manifestations which followed the criminal's execution, and for which some undefined influence that survived his physical extinction seemed, in part at least, to be responsible, I can advance no opinion.

CHAPTER I

THE CONDEMNED

When I called upon the Colonial Secretary, in the Government Offices at Melbourne, with a request that I might be allowed to visit the prisoner as he lay in jail awaiting execution, I was informed that such permission was contrary to all precedent.

I had sat directly under the eye of the culprit four weary days while the evidence accumulated that should take away his life. I had watched his varied changes of expression as the tide of testimony ebbed and flowed, and finally swelled up and overwhelmed him. I had heard against him the verdict of "the twelve good men and true" who had sat so long as arbiters of his fate, and the words of the judge condemning him to "be hanged by the neck until he was dead," and commending his soul to the mercy of a God who seemed far aloof from the scheme of human justice so long and so laboriously planned.

Short shrift had been allowed him. Condemned and sentenced on a Monday, the date for his act of expiation had been set for the early morning of the Monday then a scant three weeks away;* an appeal for a respite had been quickly and formally made, and as quickly and formally disallowed; the days granted for preparation had glided by with portentous speed, and now but five remained between him and his introduction to the gallows and the cord.

As a special and gruesome favor I had received one of the few cards issued for the execution; and it was perhaps due as much to this fact as to that of my newspaper connections (as already stated) that the Colonial Secretary finally consented to waive in my interest the usual rule of exclusion, and handed me his order for my admission to the jail. I cannot confess to any high exultation when the mandate of the Secretary, bravely stamped with the Great Seal of the Colony of Victoria, was placed in my hands—particularly as it was ac-

---

*This is in accordance with the terms of the English law in capital cases:—whereby a condemned prisoner is allowed two Sundays to live after the pronouncement of his sentence, and is executed on the morning following the second. Thus Deeming had the longest respite possible under the statute—twenty days. The shortest lease of life (fifteen days) would be allowed to a prisoner who had been sentenced on Saturday.

companied by a strict injunction that no public account should be given of the interview.

"At least," said the Colonial Secretary, "not at present. The trial has been so sensational, the crimes traced home to this unhappy man so atrocious, that popular feeling has risen to such a pitch as to make it desirable to add thereto no new occasion of excitement. Moreover, I have refused many requests similar to yours from the local newspapers; you may imagine the position I should find myself in if it became known that I had discriminated in favor of a foreign journalist—therefore I rely upon your discretion."

Thus the Colonial Secretary—in consideration of whose injunction I made no professional use of my opportunity at the time, and report upon it now only because of its relation to this present record of events. Not that I asseverate the existence of such a relation, or theorize upon it even if it were, for the sake of argument, accepted as containing the nucleus of a mystery that, after many years of consideration, remains a mystery still.

I was not alone in my visit to the condemned cell in which, heavily ironed and guarded day and night by the death-watch, Frederick Bailey

Deeming awaited his doom.* My wife, who was included in the warrant from the Colonial Secretary, accompanied me; she who had been my companion in journeys that had taken me twice around the globe, and who had shared with me many of the inexplicable experiences to which I have alluded in my "Preface;" and who, seeming throughout her life more sensitive than most of us to occult forces that at times appear to be in operation about us, has since crossed the frontier of the Undiscovered Country, there to find, perhaps, solution of some of the riddles that have perplexed both her and me. Intensely human as she was, and in all things womanly, her susceptibility to weird and uncomprehended influences must always seem a contradiction—and the more so since they always came upon her not only without invitation, but even in opposition to a will of unusual force and sanity, which, until the incidents occurred that I am about to relate, kept them measurably in control.

---

*This was the murderer's real name, as disclosed by investigations in England among relatives and acquaintances living there. His execution was, as the warrant for it recited, "upon the body of Albert Williams," this being the *alias* under which he came to Australia, as described later.

THE HAUNTED BUNGALOW

A memento of my interview with the murderer stands before me on the table as I write:—a memento also of my wife's skill in modeling, on account of which I had with difficulty induced her to be my companion on my sinister errand—an impression in plaster of his right hand; the hand against which had been proved the "deep damnation of the taking-off" of two women and four children, and in whose lines thus preserved those learned in such matters profess to discern the record of other like crimes that have been suspected of him, but could not be confirmed. I will not weary the reader with the histories that have been read to me from this grisly document, and no one now may ever know whether they be true or false:—at all events the hand that made this impress was duly found guilty of the atrocities I have recorded against it, and the price that was exacted for them will seem to none excessive, and to some a world too small.

I remember being much struck at the time with the interest which the condemned man manifested in assisting me to secure the record. My warrant from the Colonial Secretary included permission to obtain it, and the consent of the prisoner followed promptly on the asking. It came, in fact, with a sort of feverish readiness, and I fancied that his mind found in the operation some brief respite from the thoughts that his position, and the swift approach of his fate, forced upon him. He regarded with intentness the moistening of the plaster, and its manipulation into the proper degree of consistency; followed intelligently the instruction to lay his hand with even pressure upon the yielding mass, and when the cast had hardened, and was passed through the bars for his inspection, he examined it with an appearance of the liveliest satisfaction.

"Do those lines mean anything?" he asked.

"Many think so," I replied, "and even profess to read a record from them. For myself, I am ignorant of the art."

"I have heard of that," he returned. "They call it 'palmistry,' don't they? I wish you could find out whether they are going to hang me next Monday. But they'll do that, right enough. I'm thirty-nine now, and my mother always said I would die before forty. *She* died a good while ago—but she keeps coming back. She comes every night, and of late she comes in the daytime, too. What does she bother me so for? Why can't she leave me alone?" (glancing over his shoulder.) "She's here now—over there in the corner. You can't see her?

That's queer. Can't *you* see her?"—addressing the governor of the jail, who accompanied me, and who shook his head to the question. "I thought perhaps you could. But you don't miss much. She ain't pretty to look at, crying all the time and wringing her hands, and saying I'm bound to be hanged! I don't mind her so much in the daylight, but coming every night at two o'clock, and waking me up and tormenting me!—that's what I can't stand."

"Is this insanity?" I asked the governor as I came away.

"I don't know what it is," he replied. "We all thought at first it was shamming crazy, and the government sent in a lot of doctors to examine him; but he seemed sane enough when they talked with him—the only thing out about him was when he complained of his mother's visits; just as he did to you. And it is certainly true that he has a sort of fit about two o'clock every morning, and wakes up screaming and crying out that his mother is in the cell with him; and talks in a frightful, blood-curdling way to someone that nobody can see, and scares the death-watch half out of their wits. Insanity, hallucination, or an uneasy conscience—it might be any of them; I can't say. Whatever it is, it seems strange that he always talks about visitations from his mother, who, as far as I can learn, died quietly in her bed, and never of apparitions of his two wives and four children whose throats he cut with a knife held in the hand whose print you've got there under your arm. Perhaps you won't mind my saying it—but it strikes me you've got a queer taste for curiosities. I wouldn't be able to sleep with that thing in the house."

I laughed at the worthy governor's comment; yet, as it turned out, his words were pregnant with prophecy.

CHAPTER II

THE CRIME

IN the month of March, eighteen hundred and ninety-two, the people of Melbourne were startled by glaring headlines in the morning newspapers announcing the discovery of a murder in the suburb of Windsor. During the historic "boom" that started into life all manner of activities in and about the Victorian capital during the middle and later "eighties," a great stimulus to building operations had been felt, not only in the city itself, but also through all the extensive district outlying it. The suburb of Windsor enjoyed its share in this evidence of prosperity, and sanguine speculators, viewing through the glasses of a happy optimism a rush of new inhabitants to the fortunate city, erected in gleeful haste a multitude of dwellings for their purchase and occupancy. New streets were laid out across the former barren stretches of the suburb, and lined on either side by "semi-detached villas"— imposing as to name, but generally more or less "jerry-built," and exceedingly modest in their aspect.* These structures were of what we might now call a standardized pattern—housing two families side by side with a dividing partition between them, and of a single story, with an attic above. Between each two connected dwellings (which were fronted by a shallow veranda, and contained three or four rooms for each resident family) ran a narrow alley, hardly wide enough for a real separation between one building and the next, but sufficiently so to justify the description of "semi-detached" which their inventor, by a happy inspiration, had applied to them.

The "Great Melbourne Boom"—as I believe it is still referred to as distinguishing it from all other "booms," of various dimensions, which preceded or have followed it—spent its force,

* This activity in building (which is still seen in concrete form in the palatial Parliament Buildings and other costly structures of Melbourne) was largely inspired by the published calculations of an enthusiastic statistician on the future growth of the Colonies:—which were, in effect, that by 1951 their population would be thirty-two millions, and by 2001, one hundred and eighty-nine millions!—some eighty per cent in excess of that of the United States at present. It speaks loudly for Australian enterprise that these Windsor builders, as well as many others, took such prompt measures to provide for this increase.

unfortunately, before the hopes of the speculators who had ridden into Windsor on its flood had been realized; and amid the wreck and flotsam that remained to mark its ebb, some mournful miles of these "semi-detached villas" were conspicuous.

So complete was the disaster that many of the owners of these properties paid no further heed to them:—and it was with an emotion akin to surprise that, on a day in the month and year above mentioned, the agent of a certain house in Andrew street received a visit from a woman with a view to renting it. Why the prospective tenant should have selected this particular "villa" out of the scores of others precisely like it that lined both sides of this street, is not known—nor might she herself have had any definite reason for her choice. Perhaps it was Chance; perhaps Providence—the terms are possibly synonymous:—but at all events her action proved to be the first and most important of the threads that wove themselves together in a net to entrap, and bring to justice, one of the craftiest and most relentless murderers of the age.

The agent, apprised by his visitor of her desire to examine the house, eagerly prepared to accompany her, but could not find the key.

A search among his records followed; from which the fact resulted that, in the previous December, he had rented the house to a gentlemanly stranger, who, in lieu of affording references, had established confidence by paying three months' rent in advance. In the prevailing depression of the local real estate business the agent had given so little attention to his lines of empty properties that he had not since even visited the house in question—the more so as the period for which payment had been made was not yet expired. Assured by his visitor, however, that the house was certainly unoccupied, he went with her to the door, which he opened with a master-key with which he had equipped himself.

The house was in good order throughout—in fact it seemed never to have been occupied. The prospective tenant inspected it carefully and with approval, and could discover but one objection; she was sure she noticed a disagreeable odor in the parlor. Her companion (as is natural to agents with a house to dispose of) failed to detect this:—if it existed it was doubtless due to the fact that the house had been closed for some time; he would have it thoroughly aired and overhaul the drains—after which she could call again. This she agreed to do, gave the agent her name and address, and departed.

Left to himself, the agent began an investigation. With senses quickened, perhaps, by the favorable prospect of business, he became aware that the atmosphere of the parlor was undoubtedly oppressive; and as he moved about in search of the cause he observed that near the open fire-place it was positively sickening. Examining this feature of the room more carefully, he discovered that the hearth-stone had been forced up at one end, cracking and crumbling the cement in which it had been set, and from the inch-wide aperture thus formed came forth a stench so overpowering that he recoiled in horror, and gasping and strangling, staggered into the open air.

The police authorities were notified, and a mason was sent for with his tools. The hearth-stone was wrenched from its place, and in the hollow space beneath, encased in cement, knees trussed up to chin and bound with cords, lay the body of a young woman—nude save for the mantle of luxuriant dark hair that partly shrouded her, and with her throat cut from ear to ear.

About a week before Christmas of the previous year, the North German Lloyd S. S. "Kaiser Wilhelm II." from Bremen to Plymouth *via* the Suez Canal and Colombo, debarked its passengers at the port of Melbourne. Among the second-class contingent who had taken ship at Plymouth were "Albert Williams" and his wife Emily. They had not been long married, and their destination was understood by their fellow-passengers to be Colombo; but on reaching that port they remained on board and continued to Melbourne. It was remarked that Mrs. Williams, who up to that time had been the life of the company, fell thereafter under increasing fits of uneasiness and melancholy—until, at the time of arrival at Melbourne, she had drawn so far aloof from her former friends of the passage that none concerned themselves regarding her plans, or even final destination, in the new land.*

---

*This woman (*née* Emily Lydia Mather) was the daughter of John and Dove Mather, respected residents of Rainhill, a small town near Liverpool, England. To this town came Deeming, under his *alias* of "Williams," representing himself as an officer in the Indian army who had been sent to England to purchase supplies therefor. This claim he strengthened by occasionally appearing in a resplendent uniform—which seems to have been of his own invention—and reciting his many exploits "in the imminent deadly breach;" confirming also his free assertions of the possession of large wealth of his own by liberal expenditures in all directions. No such splendid personage had ever before been seen in quiet Rainhill, and the whole town succumbed to the glamor of it—including Miss Mather and her parents, whose acquaintance the fascinating officer somehow made, and followed up by a respectful but ardent courtship of the daughter. An engagement between the pair was soon announced and a valuable diamond ring, as well as other gifts of jewelry and rich attire, was bestowed by the prospective bridegroom upon the bride-to-be:—and although the celebration of the wedding was announced for so early a date as to cause some unfavorable gossip, the fact was condoned in view of the military necessity of a speedy return to India.

At this point Williams—to use the name by which he was then known—encountered what to any less bold and unscrupulous villain would have been a decided check:—this in the form of a letter from his then living legal wife, whom, with his four children by her, he had some time before deserted, and who—in some manner unknown—had now traced him to Rainhill. This letter, it is believed, announced her intention of descending upon him:—at any rate, with characteristic audacity, he gave out the information that his *sister* and her children were coming to live in Rainhill, and that he had received a letter asking him to rent a house for them. He secured a house accordingly; but expressed dissatisfaction with the somewhat worn wooden floor of the kitchen—and as the owner demurred to undertake the expense of a cement floor, Williams said he knew about such things, and would do the job himself, and ordered the necessary materials and tools. When, and by what means, the woman and children arrived in Rainhill, seems to be somewhat of a mystery:—that they *did* arrive is shown by the fact that after the Windsor murder had come to light, and the identity of the victim was discovered by a curious chain of circumstances too long to find place in this narrative, the skilfully-laid cement floor with which the old wooden floor had been replaced was torn up, and the half-decapitated bodies of the five were found embedded in it. Those who are curious in such matters may see this tragedy depicted at Madame Toussaud's, London.

No such change, however, was noted in the demeanor of her husband. He was well to the fore in all the interests and amusements that offer themselves on shipboard, rallied his wife in no very refined or considerate terms upon her growing depression, and devoted most of his spare time to a pet canary, which he had brought aboard in an elaborate gilt cage; keeping it constantly near him on deck by day, and at night sharing with it his stateroom.*

A month's association with him had not increased the liking of his fellow-voyagers. The compulsory intimacies engendered by a long journey by sea afford a trying test of character, and to it the temperament of the so-called

---

*This detail—of a murderer carrying about with him a canary as a companion—is effectively employed by the late Frank Norris in his California novel, "McTeague." As that story was published in 1903, eleven years after the execution of Deeming,—he, like McTeague, a wife-murderer,—the source of Norris' idea would seem obvious.

THE HAUNTED BUNGALOW

Albert Williams failed satisfactorily to respond. Strange and contradictory moods were noticed in him. At times he was morose and "grouchy," at times feverishly jovial and even hilarious, and the transition from one to the other of these states of mind was often startlingly abrupt. He seems, indeed, to have "got on the nerves" of all his associates on the voyage—and so at length it happened that when he went ashore, carrying the cage and canary solicitously in his hand and followed by his silent and sad-faced wife, both passengers and officers were at one in the aspiration that they might never see his sort again.

Repairing to a "Coffee-Palace"—by which sounding title temperance hotels in Australia are identified—the couple spent some days in its respectable retirement; then their belongings were entrusted to a carrying-company, and were by it conveyed to the "semi-detached villa" in Windsor. The canary, chirping and fluttering joyously in its cage, which was promptly hung in the veranda, excited for several days the mild interest of the neighbors and a few casual passers-by—but of the people in the house very little was seen. Now and then a gentleman in smoking-jacket and embroidered velvet cap was observed in the veranda, feeding and chirruping to the canary, but his companion seems to have kept herself in complete seclusion. Her murder may, indeed, have followed swiftly upon her entrance into the house; however that may be, some ten days later the canary was no longer seen in the veranda, a carrier came with his cart and took away a quantity of trunks and boxes, and as he deliberately drove away his employer kept pace with him on the sidewalk, jauntily swinging the cage with its feathered occupant in his hand.

The trunks and boxes were taken to an auction-room in Melbourne, where, after due advertisement, their contents were offered for public sale; women's garments and jewelry, for the most part, and heterogeneous odds and ends. The owner of these properties was present when the sale took place, and seemed much interested in their disposition:—but when the canary and its cage were offered he suddenly declared that he would not sell them, and when the auction closed took them away with him. He subsequently appeared in the town of Sale, several hundred miles away, and at other remote localities—perhaps with the idea of misleading possible pursuit or for some other purpose unknown:—but in all his wanderings he took the canary with him, and by his devotion to it attracted an attention to himself which had much to do with his identification when he was finally apprehended.

Returning to Melbourne, where he had before assumed the new *alias* of "Baron Swanston," he finally disposed of the cage and the canary to the auctioneer of his former acquaintance. Then he disappeared as completely as though the earth had opened and engulfed him—his crime successfully committed and unsuspected, his very name unknown, his tracks as completely covered as was the nearly decapitated body of his victim beneath the cemented hearthstone of the house at Windsor.

But even then the mysterious power of Chance—or Providence—was at work to his undoing. A peculiarity of many Australian dwellings—a peculiarity which the hastily-constructed "villas" in Windsor shared—is found in the fact that they have no cellars. This assists the work of rapid building, so important when a "boom" is on:—so the ground upon their sites had simply been levelled, a surface of cement laid, and the buildings set above it upon a layer of beams and brickwork. Nothing could be easier, under such a principle of construction, than to remove the hearth-stone, dig a grave under it through the thin layer of cement and into the soil below, conceal the body therein, restore the earth to its place, and fix the stone in position again.

What emotion the murderer may have felt when, after excavating under the cement to the depth of about eighteen inches, his tools struck upon solid rock, and he could dig no further, may be left to the imagination. Perhaps he felt no emotion whatever, not appreciating the fatal nature of this check to his plans. At all events he had no choice but to accept the situation, crowd the body into the shallow space, and by pouring cement about it and the covering hearth-stone insure the lasting secrecy of the crime. He may have been ignorant, too, of the enormous expansive power of the gases released by decomposition, which under ordinary conditions might have been absorbed by the covering and underlying soil:—here, however, with solid rock below, they struggled in their close confinement until their barrier at its weakest point gave way, and forcing up the hearth-stone disclosed to the world the horror that it had concealed.

And here is the strangest circumstance of all. Although it had been known to a few surveyors and builders, and to certain owners of buildings that had been erected, that a large part of the land on which the suburb was built rested upon a rock formation, examinations that were made subsequent to the discovery of the murder showed that at no point did this impenetrable foundation approach nearly to the surface of the soil, save under this particular house of the tragedy! Ages ago this flat table of stone had been laid down—and to the dwelling fortuitously built upon it, with hundreds of others lying empty about it for him to choose, the murderer had been guided across fifteen thousand miles of sea, there to prepare for himself detection not only for one crime, but for the other even more heinous which had so briefly preceded it.

CHAPTER III

THE FLIGHT AND CAPTURE

PROMINENT among the many commonplaces current among men is the one that "truth is stranger than fiction," and the other that Life, in building up her dreams, employs "situations" which the boldest playwright would hesitate to present upon the stage. Yet the lines that Life lays down for her productions are, in the main, closely followed by those who are ranked as among the world's greatest dramatists. She, like them, leads up to a climax by a mass of incidents that may severally be trivial, but combine together with tremendous weight; she follows farce with tragedy, and lightens tragedy with comedy; she brings her heroes in touch with clowns, her lovers with old women and comic countrymen—and in the complexities of her plots mingles them together so bewilderingly that the wonder and interest of the audience are kept vigorously alive until the curtain's fall.

So in this sordid Windsor tragedy she introduces between the first and third acts a second, where the tension is relaxed and the milder interest of Romance appears.

It was not the purpose of the murderer to remain near the scene, or even in the country, of his crime:—he was a shrewd as well as merciless villain, and he turned his face towards Sydney, evidently with the intention of taking a steamer then about to sail for San Francisco, and sinking his identity in the vast areas and amid the swarming millions of the United States.

Nemesis accompanied him, but in the disguise of Cupid. On the coastwise steamer by which he traveled to Sydney was a young woman by the name of Rounsfell, who was returning to her home in the interior of New South Wales from a visit to her brother near the border-line between Victoria and South Australia. She was about eighteen years of age, and from an interview I later had with her I estimated her as an attractive and modest girl, not strikingly intellectual, but of kindly disposition and affectionate nature. To her the fugitive, introducing himself by his latest-assumed name, paid regardful court, and relieved the tedium of the voyage by devoted attentions; and when the boat arrived at Sydney, where she was to remain a few days, he escorted her to one hotel and saw to her satisfactory accommodation, while he himself, with admirable delicacy, took up quarters at another. During her stay he continued his attentions with equal respect and assiduity; his attitude, as she told me afterward, was more like that of an elder brother than a lover—this attitude being confirmed by judicious advice and counsel, and even by moral admonition:—as when he gently chided her for her confessed fondness for dancing, sagely implying that he regarded this form of amusement as one of the most insidious wiles of the Adversary.

It was at Coogee, on the shores of the beautiful harbor of Sydney, that this chaste and improving courtship culminated in his asking her to marry him. He was a man of wealth, he told her, a mining engineer by profession, and with several lucrative positions in Australia at the moment waiting upon his selection. To these practical considerations he added the plea of his devotion. He had "lately lost his wife" (delicate euphemism!) he said, and stirred her sympathies by eloquent and tearful descriptions of the lonely and unsatisfactory life he led in consequence of this bereavement—the hollowness of which life he felt more acutely than ever now that she had crossed his path. She was, as I have said, a tender-hearted girl, and what more natural than that she should willingly incline her ear to words which every woman loves to hear?—the more so when they were uttered by a man whose history indicates him to have inherited all the persuasiveness of the original Serpent in dealings with the sex, and who, as my interview with him in the condemned cell caused me to remark, possessed one of the sweetest and most sympathetic voices I ever heard in human throat.

It would be no discredit to Miss Rounsfell if she had accepted him then and there; but it speaks well for her prudence and self-command that she asked for delay in giving her answer until she could lay the matter before her parents. To this he promptly assented, adding the suggestion that he should accompany her to her home, and give her friends an opportunity to become acquainted with him. This plan was carried out, and the successful conquest of the daughter was completed by the capitulation of the family; the engagement was formally announced, and the joyful contract sealed by the installation upon the hand of the *fiancée* of the costly diamond ring so lately worn by the woman whose mutilated body was at the moment mouldering under the hearth-stone at Windsor.

The ecstasy of the betrothal inspired a consideration of ways and means to hasten the wedding. The ardent lover pleaded for the celebration of the nuptials without further ado; but his more prudent mistress urged the possession of a home, and definite employment as surety of maintaining it. This point conceded, the question arose as to what particular section of the Colonies seemed to offer the most attractive opportunities. The bride-elect objected to New South Wales as being too near home (she had always been a home-body, and wished to see the world); Victoria, also, was not to her taste for some other feminine but conclusive reason; Western Australia had just begun to come into notice as likely to become one of the world's greatest gold-producers—there, it seemed to her, was the land of promise for a young and experienced mining-engineer.

This opinion prevailed, and the fugitive, abandoning any idea he may have had of escaping to America, set out for the new El Dorado; and in a few weeks his *fiancée* was cheered by a letter giving news of his arrival at Southern Cross—a mining-camp some hundred and fifty miles in the interior—where he had secured the post of manager for a company which owned a rich deposit, and where he was already preparing for her coming. Thus some weeks passed, until another letter came informing her that a house had been secured and fitted up for her, and enclosing sufficient funds for her journey. She replied, fixing the date of her departure from Sydney, and on the day appointed took train for Melbourne, intending to continue thence to Albany by sea.

Arriving at Melbourne the following morning—where by chance she took a room in the same "Coffee Palace" to which her prospective bridegroom had resorted upon his arrival from England—she despatched a note to a young man who was a long-time friend of her family, and when he called in the evening went out with him for a stroll through the city. As they passed the office of *The Age* newspaper on Collins street, they saw an excited crowd surrounding the bulletin-board, and crossed the roadway to read the announcement that it bore. As her eyes rested upon it, Miss Rounsfell gave a piercing shriek, and fell senseless upon the ground.

The announcement upon the board was this:

"BARON SWANSTON, THE WINDSOR MURDERER, ARRESTED AT SOUTHERN CROSS."

Taken to her hotel and revived with difficulty, she told her sensational story, with which the newspapers of the whole country were filled next day; then, broken and trembling, she returned to her home, there to remain until summoned again to Melbourne to give her testimony at the trial which took place a month later.

Most strangely had it happened that by her unwitting influence the criminal career of Frederick Bailey Deeming had been brought to an end. Had she consented to live, after her anticipated marriage, in New South Wales or Victoria, he might never have been apprehended. In these two colonies—except for the seeming impossibility of the murdered body being discovered—he might have come and gone without suspicion; his only peril being the almost negligible one that some associate of his voyage from England, or one of the very few persons in Melbourne who had seen him with his former wife, might encounter him and inquire as to his changed name and partner:—but the extrication of himself from such an entanglement would have been merely a stimulating mental exercise to Deeming, whose record, as searched after his latest crime was known and the hue-and-cry was on his trail, shows him to have been a most accomplished swindler, and a man of singular address in all forms of deceit.

In these comparatively populous sections, too, the free and wide circulation of newspapers would have brought immediate warning, by announcement of the discovery of the Windsor murder, of the danger he was in, and thus have aided his escape; for it was not until several days after the body was found that its identity was revealed, and many more before any clue was found to Deeming's whereabouts. With railways extending to ports in New South Wales, Victoria, South Australia and Queensland, his opportunities for quitting the country quickly and secretly were numerous; and once away before the search for him had even been started, the chance of capturing him would have been poor indeed.

In Western Australia, whither Miss Rounsfell had been innocently instrumental in sending him, the situation was entirely different. No railways connect the colony with the others, and ingress and egress are alike possible only by sea. Moreover, being the latest of the Colonies in which the old English system of penal-transportation was abolished, and still harboring many of the former subjects of that *régime,* Western Australia at this time maintained through its police a close system of espionage over all who arrived or departed by the few seaports of the district. Thus did the murderer walk into a *cul-de-sac;* and when the pursuit (by an extraordinarily sagacious piece of deductive work on the part of the Melbourne detectives, which it would interfere with the purpose of this narrative to describe) reached Albany, the officers, armed with warrants for his arrest and learning from the local police records that a man such as they described had "gone up country" and had not returned, had only to endure the tedious desert journey to Frazer's gold-mines at Southern Cross, and apprehend him in the very house he had prepared for his awaited bride.

CHAPTER IV

THE EXPIATION

RUN to earth, and captured like a rabbit at the end of its burrow, the murderer was brought to Albany, and shipped to Melbourne by the liner "Ballaarat." As a relief from the general lack of events of interest that marked his return progress, it may be noted that the train on which he traveled from Freemantle to Albany, was stormed at York by an indignant populace, who voiced the sentiment universally pervading all the Colonies against his atrocities by a determined effort to visit a rude, if original, form of justice upon him by tearing him to pieces between two bullock-teams, and were dissuaded with difficulty from this intention by a display of revolvers by his guards. His feelings were outraged also on the steamer, where he expressed himself as much distressed by the light and profane conversation of certain unregenerate marines who were on their way to the Australian station, and strongly rebuked them therefor:—thus illustrating anew the strange contradiction in his nature which was before shown in his reproach of Miss Rounsfell's fondness for dancing. In fact, all who at various times came in contact with him—including and ending with his guardians in the Melbourne jail—remarked upon his scrupulousness of language and nicety of conduct.

I have gone thus at some length into a description of this monster and his crimes for two reasons:—in the first place because it seemed essential to show the causes of the repulsion and horror which his very name inspired, and thus to place the reader in a position to appreciate the effect upon the popular mind of later incidents which I am about to record; and, in the second place, because the close study which I was able to give alike to the man and his deeds convinced me that his case was one possessing far more interest for the psychologist than even the criminologist.

The ingenious Sir William S. Gilbert, in the song of the sentimental police sergeant in "The Pirates of Penzance," wherein it is recited that

> "When the enterprizing burglar isn't burgling,
> When the cutthroat isn't occupied with crime,
> He loves to hear the little brook a-gurgling,
> And listens to the merry village chime"—

THE HAUNTED BUNGALOW

voiced a truth which has been marked in the cases of many malefactors. It has been observed of Deeming that, in the intervals of swindling, lying and homicide by which his career is chiefly remembered, he bristled like a copybook with virtuous and noble sentiments— nor is his sincerity to be doubted in their utterance. It is unquestionable that he was a man of singular address and subtlety—not only among men skilled in business affairs and experienced in reading character. He was a clever mechanic, and able to adapt himself quickly and efficiently to any occupation:—as is shown by the fact that although there is nothing in his history to indicate that he had had any previous experience in mine-management, he more than fulfilled all the requirements laid upon him at Southern Cross, increased the output of gold by ingenious inventions, and was esteemed by the company as the most capable manager it had ever had. He had a marked, if imperfectly developed, fondness for music and literature, and although his conversation included many grammatical solecisms, it was effective and often eloquent. His taste in dress, although rather flamboyant in the matter of jewelry, of which he always wore a profusion, was noticeably correct—the frock-coat, light trousers and perfectly-fitting patent-leather shoes which he wore at his trial were evidently from the hands of the best London outfitters, and would have graced (as they doubtless had done) the fashionable afternoon parade which is a feature of Melbourne's Collins Street.

The anomaly that is suggested by these established facts regarding him is of minor interest, however, in comparison with more striking contradictions that were remarked after his capture. It was my fortune to have a place near him at the inquest which resulted in his commitment for trial, as well as at the trial itself that duly followed. Popular feeling against him was so intense and violent that the authorities did not dare to land him at the steamboat pier, but smuggled him aboard a tug when the "Ballaarat" entered the harbor, and brought him ashore at the suburb of St. Kilda, whence he was hurried in a closed cab to the Melbourne jail. Brought into the court where the inquest was held, his appearance was so brutal and revolting that a murmur of horror and disgust arose at his entrance which the judge and officers with difficulty quelled.

There was in his deeply-lined and saturnine face no indication of an understanding of his position. His lips were drawn in a sardonic sneer, and his eyes—steely, evil and magnetic—glistened like those of the basilisk as he looked boldly and with a sort of savage bravado at the faces about him. He disdained to pay any attention to the proceedings, and was seemingly deaf to the testimony that was advanced against him by more than thirty witnesses. Yet he evinced a lively, if contemptuous, interest in minor details, and audibly expressed his views regarding them. When the canary that had played so singular a part in his Australian experiences was produced, still in its ornate gilded cage, he cried out: "Hullo! here comes the menagerie! Why don't the band play?" Of a reporter taking notes at a table near him he remarked that "he wrote like a hen," commented upon the weak utterance of a certain witness that "he had no more voice than a consumptive shrimp," and interjected ribald criticisms on the words of the judge that were fairly shocking under the circumstances.

When, at the termination of the proceedings, the judge ordered his commitment for trial, and stated that a rescript would be issued against him for the wilful murder of his wife, Emily Williams, he shouted, in a shrill, cackling, strident sort of voice: "And when you have got it, you can put it in your pipe and smoke it!"—looking about with a demoniac grin as if expecting applause for an effective bit of repartee. As the constables seized him and dragged him to the door, his eyes fell upon a comely young woman standing on the edge of the crowd, who regarded him with horrified amazement. Breaking away from the officers, he danced up to her, chucked her under the chin, and with his leering face close to hers ejaculated: "O, you ducky, ducky!" and disappeared amid the cries of the scandalized lookers-on.

I do not know what the emotions of other attendants on the trial may have been, but I remember my own mental attitude as one of distaste that my duties as a correspondent required my presence. To see one weak human being contending for his life against the organized and tremendous forces of the Law is always a pitiful and moving spectacle; in this case, with recollections of the repulsive incidents of the inquest in mind, one nerved oneself for some scene of desperation and horror. The dock, surrounded by a spiked railing and already guarded by a posse of white-helmeted constables, stood in the centre of the court-room, its platform, elevated some three feet from the floor, being furnished with a trapdoor that communicated with the cells below by a spiral iron staircase, which the prisoner must ascend. The audience watched this trap-door in somewhat that state of hesitating eagerness with which a child awaits the spring of a jack-in-the-box, not knowing what grotesque or terrifying thing may appear:—and when it lifted, and the murderer stepped to his place beneath the thousand-eyed gaze that was fastened upon him, a murmur in which amazement was the dominant note ran through the room.

My own first feeling was that my eyesight was playing me a trick; my second, that by some change of program of which I had not been informed, the trial of Deeming had been postponed. In this frock-coated, well-groomed and gentlemanly person in the dock there was no trace whatever of the ruffian who had been the central figure of the inquest. In age he seemed to have dropped some twenty years; his manner was perfect, showing no trace either of apprehension or bravado:—in short, the impression he conveyed (as I described it in my correspondence at the time) was of a young clergyman of advanced views presenting himself to trial for heresy, rather than of one of the most brutal murderers of his generation.

This impression prevailed during the four days his trial lasted; only once or twice could one detect in his eye the former flash of implacableness and ferocity. It was not as if he made an effort to keep himself in control, but rather as if he were a man with two strongly opposed and antagonistic sides to his nature, of which one or the other might manifest itself without any conscious exercise of will.

It was also evident to anyone who could observe him dispassionately that the details of the murder, as they were brought out in the testimony, were all as news to *him*:—and when, in the address he made to the jury before it retired to consider its verdict, he admitted knowledge of the subsidiary facts brought out (as to his acquaintance with Miss Rounsfell, for example), but swore he was as innocent as he was incapable of the murder of his wife, I, for one, believed him sincere, although I could perceive in the faces about me that I was alone in that opinion. A suggestion that this man might illustrate the phenomenon of "dual personality" and should be subjected to hypnotic suggestion at the hands of qualified experts, rather than have swift condemnation measured out to him, would doubtless have been received with derision by the hard-headed audience that was the real jury in the case; but I felt at the time, and feel now even more strongly, that if Frederick Bailey Deeming had been tried in a country where psychological aberrations have been the subject of study, he would have been committed, not to the hangman, but to a lifelong restraint wherein science might have gained from his extraordinary personality much valuable knowledge.

The man whose life was choked out of him on the gallows three weeks later was the man of the inquest, not the man of the trial—and in this fact is some occasion for satisfaction. He was more subdued, as though he appreciated—as any other animal might do—what the sinister preparations for his ending meant:— but when, as he hung beneath the open trap, the death-cap was lifted from his face, there were plainly to be seen the hard and brutal lines about his mouth, and the wolfish sneer upon his lips, which one could not but feel, with something like a shudder, had distinguished his features in the commission of the atrocities for which at last he had paid such insufficient price as society could exact.

The scaffold of the Melbourne jail is a permanent structure with several traps; and across and above it runs a heavy beam, its ends fixed in the solid masonry of the walls, and the greater part of its length scarred and grooved by the chafing of the ropes which, from time to time, have given despatch to the souls of several hundred murderers. As I looked up at this fearsome tally-stick, I turned to the oldest warder of the jail, a man of nearly seventy years, who had been present at my interview with Deeming a few days before, and who now stood beside me.

"I want to ask you a question," I said, "unless your official position may prevent your answering it."

"What is it, sir?" he inquired.

"You have been for many years a warder here, and must have seen many men under sentence of death."

"Yes," he replied. "I was first here in the bushranging days, and have been here ever since. I fancy I have seen two hundred men depart this life by the route of that gallows."

"Then," said I, "you should be a good judge of the character and mental state of a man who is awaiting a death of that sort. Here is my question:—What is your opinion of Deeming?"

"Mad, sir," replied the warder. "Mad as a March hare."

This verdict might be qualified, but I believe it to be essentially just.

CHAPTER V

THE HOUSE ON THE HILL

IN beginning this chapter I find myself facing a dilemma—one not so puzzling as that which gave Hamlet pause, and evoked his famous soliloquy, and yet like it, too, in that it forces me to hesitate before the mystery of the Unseen. Thus far my story has the support of incontrovertible facts and permanent and referable legal and criminal records; I must now cut loose from these, and trust my weight upon the assertion that the last half of my narrative, which I now launch upon, is in every detail and particular as true as the first. In the stress of the responsibility thus assumed it might seem natural to marshall about me such facts and persons as I might invoke as corroborative witnesses. Of these there are not a few:—but although there is (sometimes) "wisdom in a multitude of counsellors," conviction in the actuality of truth in narrations of so-called "supernatural" phenomena is as likely as otherwise to be befogged in exact proportion to the size of their "cloud of witnesses." Therefore I have, after reflection, decided to "take the stand" myself and unsupported, and to throw myself upon the mercy of the court—my readers—in so doing.

Thus, then, I shall not reveal the exact location of The House on the Hill, nor the name of the owner, from whom, for a year, I rented it. It is doubtful that he be now living, for he was a man of advanced age when he left his house in my hands, and departed with his two unmarried daughters (themselves of mature years) for a twelve-months' tour in Europe. On his return I handed him the keys without any reference to the strange occurrences that had come to me from my bargaining with him: —nor do I know to this day whether he had similar experiences after my departure, or even whether they may have enlivened him and his family prior to my tenancy. His evident anxiety to lease the house for a time (I took it furnished, and at a rental absurdly low—in fact, just one-half his original demand) may have had no special significance, although I often fancied afterwards that I had found a reason for it:—but on consideration I decided not to refer to certain features of the house that he had failed to enumerate as among its attractions, and to restore him without remark to their renewal—if he knew of them—or to discover them for himself—if he did not.

It is probable that few of my readers have spent a year in a "haunted house"—I use this expression, although it defines nothing, for want of a better:—but those who cherish such an experience will understand why, on the one hand, I did not wish to alarm an elderly gentleman and his amiable daughters, or "give a bad name," as the saying is, to his property; and why, on the other, I did not care to run the risk of living in his recollection, and in the minds of his neighbors to whom he might relate my story, as a person of feeble intellect, if not a lunatic outright. But I would give a good deal to know what *he* knew about that house.

A circumstance that I took no note of at the time, but which afterwards seemed to have a possible significance, occurred at the house one evening when I had called to complete negotiations by signing the lease and going through other formalities precedent to taking possession. The owner had told me that one of his reasons for desiring a change of scene for a time was that his wife had died three months before after a lingering illness that had completely worn out his daughters as well as himself:—and when the business of his final evening was completed, the younger woman uttered this strange remark:—"Well, it will be a relief not to see mother about all the time!"—and was immediately checked by her sister. I had before noted her as a nervous-mannered, somewhat anæmic-looking person, and her observation touched my mind too lightly to leave any impression upon it.

There was nothing at all peculiar in the appearance of the house. It stood upon a breezy hill-top in the outskirts of one of Melbourne's most attractive suburbs; the train from town landed me, every evening, at the village station, and a ten-minute walk up a rather steep road brought me comfortably to home and dinner. The house was a delightful one when you got to it. It occupied a corner lot, and had extensive grounds around it; there was a large orchard at the rear, filled with grape-vines, and pear, lemon, and fig trees—although none of them did much in the matter of bearing. There were two trees in the front yard that gave profusely of pomegranates (a decorative fruit, but one whose edible qualities always seemed to me greatly overrated); there were spacious flower beds on both sides of the building, and the nearest neighbors were at least two hundred yards away. On the other side of the street which ran in front of the house was a large, unimproved lot which gave a touch of the country by the presence in it of several ancient gum trees, in which the "laughing jackasses" cackled and vociferated both morning and evening:— and when my wife and I, and the gentleman of Scottish ancestry and of advanced middle-age, whom, as our best of friends, we had induced to share the enterprise with us, looked about upon these things on the first afternoon of our occupancy, we pronounced them all "very good."

The house was not a large one, comprising six living-rooms and a kitchen, besides a bath and a commodious storeroom and pantry. It was of the bungalow pattern, a type which is a favorite one in Australia, where the high average temperature of the year makes coolness and airiness prime essentials in a dwelling. It had no cellar, but was raised above the ground upon brickwork, thus forming a dry air-chamber below, and above its single story was a low, unfinished attic, which afforded another air-space, and stretched without partitions from front to back of the house. There was no floor to this attic, and on the only occasion when I explored it, I had to crawl from beam to beam, the pointed roof being so low that I could barely stand upright even under its ridgepole. The only means of access to this part of the house was a ladder, which could be brought into the bathroom, and from which could be raised a light trap-door in the ceiling. A veranda ran along the front of the house, and a wide hall extended, without turn or obstruction, from front to back. On one side of this hall—beginning from the veranda—were the parlor, dining-room, bedroom, and pantry; on the other, my wife's bedroom, the bathroom, our friend's room, a "spare-room," and the kitchen:—while a few yards behind the house stood a one-story structure, fitted up as a laundry. The "spare-room" here mentioned I furnished as a smoking-room; and further equipped it by building a bench across the space before the single window, whereat I employed myself now and then in preparing the skins of birds of which I was making a collection, and which I either shot myself in frequent excursions into the country, or which were sent to me by agents, both whites and "blackfellows," whom I employed in various parts of the Colonies.

One, and perhaps the most peculiar, feature of the bungalow remains to be described. This was a small apartment, about five feet square, between the bathroom and our friend's room (but without any means of direct communication with either), and entered only by a narrow door which swung outward into the hall. It was unlighted, and was provided with air by a ventilator at the end of a shaft which was carried through the ceiling into the attic and ended in the roof. Its floor was of thickly-laid concrete, and in its centre, and occupying nearly the whole ground space, was a sunken portion about two feet deep, and equipped with wooden racks upon which boxes of butter, pans of milk, and various receptacles containing similar perishable articles of food were accommodated. This chamber was of real use in a country where —at the time at least—ice was scarce and expensive, and where summer temperatures of a hundred and ten degrees in the shade might be expected; since, being placed in a part of the house which was wholly removed from the direct rays of the sun, the air in it was always cool and dry. I am particular in describing this room because of a strange incident that later occurred in it.

The house was well, almost luxuriously, furnished. The parlor contained a fine piano, and several pictures of merit adorned the walls; heat (seldom necessary in that mild climate except on rainy days in autumn and winter) was furnished to this and other rooms by open fireplaces, and vases and other *bric-a-brac* stood upon the mantels; the bed and table linen was all of excellent quality, there was a sufficiency of crockery and glass and silverware and culinary utensils:—and as we sat down to our inauguratory dinner, and contrasted our condition with the three years' previous experience of travel and steamer and hotel life in all parts of Australia, New Zealand, Tasmania and the Fiji Islands, we congratulated each other that we had found a "home" indeed.

We set about forthwith to improve our temporary property. On one side of the house, and separated from it by a fence that inclosed the lawn and flower gardens, was a grassy "paddock" that might formerly have pastured a horse or a cow. As we had no use for either of these animals, we turned this space into a poultry yard, and populated it with chickens, ducks and geese—which thrived amazingly, and in due time furnished us all the eggs and poultry required for our table. Our friend (by nature and early training an ardent horticulturist, but whose energies in that science had for many years enjoyed no opportunity for exercise in the soil of the Melbourne Stock Exchange, of which he was a member) joyously took the flower gardens under his control, and achieved miracles therein. It was delightful, as I sat in the shady veranda on the hot Saturday afternoons, with a steamer chair to loll in, and a pipe and cooling drink at hand, to contemplate his enthusiasm as he delved and sweated to prepare new ground for the gorgeous blooms which he coaxed from the willing soil—at the same time extolling my own sagacity in asking him to share the place with us; to which he would respond in appropriate language. Our household was so small that we were not exposed to the annoyances of the "servant-girl" problem:—our friend and I lunched in town, and a capable woman who lived nearby assisted my wife in cooking and serving our dinners, and attended to the duties of house-cleaning—returning to her own home when her work was accomplished, and leaving us to ourselves in the evenings. We were near enough to town to run in for theatres and concerts whenever we were so minded, and on Sundays did some modest entertaining:—in short, we settled into a phase of existence as nearly

Arcadian as is often possible under modern conditions of civilization, and although it seemed likely to be commonplace and uneventful, we were in mood to find it all the more desirable and pleasant on that account. That the most startling experiences of our lives were soon to come upon us never entered our heads, and for some six weeks we lived in serenity and happiness amid surroundings that day by day grew more attractive.

CHAPTER VI

ON THE WINGS OF THE STORM

MY interview with the murderer, as described in the first chapter, took place upon a Thursday. The next day was one of the general holidays that are so profusely celebrated in Australia:—I do not remember the occasion, but it is safe to assume that some important horse race was to be run at Flemington—the Epsom of the Antipodes. At all events, I took advantage of the opportunity to go into the country with my gun on a collecting trip, and returned at night with a fine assortment of cockatoos, parrots and other brilliantly plumaged or curious birds which make the Colonies a paradise for the ornithologist.

The day following—Saturday—opened with a heavy rain, and a strong wind off the sea. I had no particular business to call me to town, and, anyhow, all activities and occupations would cease at noon in deference to the usual weekly half-holiday. Moreover, I had several hours' work before me in removing and preserving the skins of the birds I had shot; so I suppressed the faint voice of duty that suggested that I might find something of importance awaiting me in Melbourne, and after breakfast sat down to the congenial labor of my taxidermist's bench. Our friend departed for the Stock Exchange, and my wife and I were left alone in the house.

I had no more than made the preliminary incision in the breast of a purple lorrikeet when the doorbell rang. Answering the summons I found in the veranda a black-haired, sallow-faced individual, his garments sodden with rain, who offered for my purchase and perusal "The History and Last Confession of Frederick Bailey Deeming," for "the small price of sixpence." More in commiseration for the wretched and bedraggled appearance of the vendor than from any other motive (for I was already acquainted with the "History," and gave no credence to any announcement that a "Confession" had been made) I bought the pamphlet and returned to my room. Finding, as I had suspected, that this piece of literature contained no new facts whatever, and was totally lacking in anything even the most remotely suggesting confession, I threw it into the fire that blazed on the hearth and took up my interrupted work.*

The incident of the water-soaked vendor and his pamphlet had had the effect, however, of turning my reflections into a very unpleasant channel. In spite of all efforts to apply myself to the task in hand, the thought of the despairing man in the condemned cell, my visit to him two days before, and my anticipated presence at his execution within forty-eight hours, pressed upon my spirit with a weight which I found it impossible to lift. An incident which had occurred on the previous day had also added a certain element of pathos to the situation.

*I had good personal reasons for discrediting any rumor that Deeming had made confession, for the reason that, with the sanction of the authorities in his case, and assisted by his own counsel, I had made every effort to secure it myself—and had failed. When the matter was suggested to Deeming, and he was assured that the money that was offered to him for his memoirs would be paid to Miss Rounsfell as some slight recognition of the wrong he had done her, he eagerly assented; and being supplied with pens (quill—for not the least article in steel was allowed him) he went to work, and in a few days had turned out a large amount of manuscript. Examination of it, however, was disappointing. It began encouragingly, and there were lucid passages in it; but as a whole it was utterly incoherent—and to those who had dispassionately studied the man, an undoubted proof of his insanity.

During my absence a letter had come to my wife through the morning mail, which, to her astonishment and disquiet, proved to have been written by the murderer. It ran as follows:

"H. M. Gaol
"Melbourne
"18-5-92

"Dear Madam:
"I beg to tender you my sincere thanks for your extreme kindness on my behalf, in trying to get Miss Rounsefell to come and see me. I assure you that if she had come I could have died happy, as it is I shall die most unhappy. I am very sorry indeed that you did not find her as kind and as Christian like as yourself. Again thanking you,
 "I beg to remain
  "Most respectfully yours
   "B. Swanston.

"you may show Miss Rounsefell this if you wish. B. S."

This remarkable document, from a man at the moment standing on the brink of eternity, greatly disturbed (as I have said) its recipient; but she did not hesitate. As the letter intimates, she had already, in pursuance of a promise she was almost compelled to make through the earnest plea of the murderer when she saw him in the condemned cell, seen Miss Rounsfell (this is the correct spelling of the name, not that used by the writer of the above letter) with the lack of success that the letter suggests. Now, however, she determined to see the girl again:—and showing her the letter, she urged her to see the man—or at the least write to him—and grant her pardon to a dying creature who seemed to have no hope of pardon elsewhere, either here or hereafter. The interview was a touching one:—Miss Rounsfell was deeply affected, and (greatly to her credit, I think) consented to undertake in person the charitable mission that she had been asked to perform. But her brother so strenuously opposed the idea—even to the minor extent of writing—that she was compelled to abandon it; and Deeming went to his death without the consolation that he had so simply and eloquently craved.

Thus in many ways I had been brought into this tragical affair much more intimately than I liked, and I could not keep my mind away from it. The day itself added to the gloom that fell upon me. The storm had steadily increased in violence since early morning; rain fell in torrents, and the wind roared and whined alternately about the house; the heavy clouds that passed close overhead cast upon the earth a series of shifting shadows as their substance thickened or thinned under the rending force of the gale—if the Powers of Darkness ever walk abroad by day, they could hardly find an occasion more eerie and fitting than this. Yet no such suggestion occurred to me: —I could hear the rattle of dishes in the kitchen and the voice of my wife in song as she attended to her household duties; I lighted my pipe as another means of affording the companionship that I somehow craved, and for an hour or so applied myself assiduously to the task in hand.

I was seated facing the window, my back to the open door that led into the hall. Suddenly, and without the slightest warning, I heard behind me a long and dismal groan. "A-a-ah!"—thus it came; a woman's voice, apparently, and with an indescribable but certain accent in it of mental or physical pain. It is no exaggeration to say that this awful and ghastly sound froze me where I sat; I could feel my hair move upon my scalp, and a chill, as though I had been dashed with ice-water, ran up and down my spine. For a moment an inexpressible horror possessed me—then I felt my blood, which seemed on the instant to have stopped in its course, flow again in my veins, and with a mighty effort I arose and faced the open door. There was nothing there—nor in the dim hall, into which I shortly ventured:— I removed my slippers and silently explored every room; still nothing to be seen, and the only sound the splash of rain, and of the wind that sobbed and muttered around the house. I crept to the kitchen and peeped in cautiously: —my wife was quietly engaged in her work, and I was glad to think that she had heard nothing. Indeed, her undisturbed demeanor encouraged the opinion I had begun to form, that some peculiar effect of the wind in the open fireplace or the chimney of my room was responsible for the sound I had heard.

Yet I was by no means satisfied with this explanation:—the cry was too human, the distress it evidenced too poignant, to be thus counterfeited, and as I returned to my bench, it was with full expectation that I should hear it again. I was not disappointed. In a few moments it came, more distinct and lugubrious than before, and seemingly within the very room itself; and as I whirled about to confront I knew not what, the groan was repeated, coming from the empty air before me and dying away in an unutterably sad and plaintive sigh.

I made another swift and noiseless survey of the house, but it was as resultless as before, and regained my room much shaken, I will confess, but still unwilling to admit that the sounds could not be referred to natural causes. But I found no solution that convinced me. I might have attributed their first occurrence to hallucination, but the second hearing weakened that hypothesis—the groan and the following sigh were inimitably those of an old woman, who was either at the point of death or overwhelmed with distress of mind and body. This resemblance was absolute, and I sat for some time revolving the strange thing in my mind. I thought of relating my experience to my wife, but feared to alarm her, and finally went back to my birds.

Almost immediately there came for the third time that ghastly wail and sigh—so close to my ear that, had any living person uttered them, his face must almost have touched my own. I am not ashamed to say that the effect upon me was so unmanning and terrible that I uttered a cry of horror and fell backward with the chair I sat in, and lay sprawling on the floor. At the same instant I heard my wife scream from the kitchen; and as I gathered myself up and ran to her, I saw her standing with her back against the wall, staring with horrified eyes, and with a look of repulsion and fear upon her face, at something invisible to me, on the other side of the room. I rushed to her and grasped her hands:—they were cold as ice, and her fixed and rigid gaze into what to me was emptiness, frightened me beyond measure.

"In heaven's name," I cried, "what is it?"

"It is Deeming's mother," she answered, in a whisper I could hardly hear.

"Deeming's mother!"—I echoed her words:—"How do you know it is Deeming's mother?"

"I saw her with him in his cell at the jail," she replied.

"Then what he said was true, that his mother comes back to trouble him?"

"Yes, it *was* true; and now she comes to *me!* Go away!" she cried, addressing something *I* could not see. "I cannot help you; why do you torment me! Ah!"—with a sigh of relief—"she has gone!" and she sank exhausted into a chair.

We had a long and memorable talk after that, which I will briefly summarize. My wife had not heard the groans that had been audible to me until their second repetition; then the sound that had seemed beside my ear came at the same instant close to hers, and her cry that joined with mine had been wrung from her by the sight of the apparition which on the instant presented itself to her. This was not the first time, however, that it had appeared:—it had closely followed upon the receipt of Deeming's letter the day before, and its cries of distress and appeals for help had been so agonizing that it was as much on that account as because of the plea of the murderer himself that she had decided to see Miss Rounsfell again.

The apparition did not reappear that day, and there was no recurrence of the wailing lamentations—but we were soon to have further experience of them for all that.

The storm spent itself during the late afternoon, and was succeeded by a beautiful evening. The wind was still high, and the sky filled with broken masses of clouds, through which the full moon waded heavily:—and as my wife and I descended the hill, soon after dinner, to the railway station on our way to keep an engagement to call upon the Consul-General of the United States at his residence at St. Kilda, we agreed that the night was just such a one as might inspire Doré in some one of his fantastic compositions. After the day's gruesome events we had hesitated about leaving our friend alone during our absence; but we finally united upon the opinion which my wife advanced, that as she seemed to be the sole object of the apparition's visit, he was not likely to be molested. So we left him (albeit with some misgiving) comfortably seated before the dining-room fire in a large easy-chair, and with his pipe and a new novel for company, and took our departure.

It was after midnight when we returned. The gale had blown itself out, and the moon looked down upon a world that seemed resting in sleep after the turmoil of the day. My wife went at once to her room to lay aside her outer garments and I repaired, with much curiosity and a little apprehension stirring me, to the dining-room.

I found our friend as we had left him, book in hand and with his smoked-out pipe lying on a table beside him. He was not alone, however—our two dogs—a wire-haired Scotch terrier and a fox-terrier—which I had as usual chained up for the night in their kennels at the back of the house, were dozing together on the hearth-rug.

"Hullo!" I exclaimed; "what are those dogs doing here? You know they are never allowed to come into the house."

"Well," our friend replied. "I felt lonely, and so I brought them in to keep me company."

"That's an odd idea," I rejoined. "I thought your book and pipe would be society enough. Besides, there is plenty of 'Scotch' and soda on the sideboard."

"I tried that, too," he confessed. "But, do you know? this has been the most infernally unpleasant evening I ever spent in my life. The wind has been making the most uncanny noises —I would swear there were people moving all over the house if I did not know I was the only person in it. I have been all over the place a dozen times, but could find nothing. At last I couldn't stand it; so I unchained and brought in the dogs. Somehow they didn't seem to have much use for the place—I had to drag them in by their collars."

"They knew they had no right to be here," I commented. "The matter with *you* is, you've been smoking too much, and got your nerves on edge. Come and help me put up the dogs before my wife sees them, or you'll 'get what for,' as your English expression is."

This office performed, we returned to the

dining-room, where I suggested a "Scotch-and-soda" before retiring for the night, and together at the sideboard we prepared each a modest potion. As we touched glasses to a good sleep and happy awakening, there sounded from the air behind us that weird and terrible cry! My friend's face turned ashen on the instant and his glass fell from his hand and lay shattered on the hardwood floor.

"My God!" he cried; "did you hear *that?*"

I was startled, of course, but the morning's experience, reinforced by anticipation of some such happening, had steeled my nerves.

"Did I hear *what?*" I asked. "Look here, old man, you are certainly in a queer way tonight. What *should* I hear?—everything is as quiet as death."

"Do you mean to tell me," he demanded, looking at me incredulously and with alarm still in his face, "that you did not hear that awful groan?"—but meanwhile I had filled another tumbler for him, which he hastily emptied, although the glass rattled against his teeth as he drank.

"Come, come!" I said; "go to bed, and you will be all right in the morning;"—but the words had but left my lips when, right between us as it seemed, there swelled again upon the air that utterance of anguish, followed by the dying cadence of a sigh.

"There!—there!—there!" stammered my companion:—"did you hear it *then?*"

"Yes, I did," I replied; "and the first time as well. Is that what has disturbed you tonight?"

"No, not exactly that—nothing so awful; but all sorts of strange noises; I can't describe them. I say—what kind of a house *is* this? I have always believed the stories of haunted houses were bally nonsense; but in heaven's name what does all this mean?"

I was unable to enlighten him:—and although I called my wife from her room and described to him our morning's experience with the voices, I thought it best to keep the feature of the apparition a secret. In fact, he never did learn of it, or of many other things that did not come directly to his personal apprehension. What he *did* see and hear, in the months that followed, was bad enough, God knows!—and I am convinced that one of the reasons (and that not the least considerable) which prevented him from leaving us on any one of a dozen different occasions, and ourselves from abandoning the house outright, was the consideration (on his part) that it would be unseemly for one of his nation to confess himself inferior in pluck to an American, and (on ours) that we should be untrue to all our country's traditions if we permitted a Britisher to see us in retreat.

This reason may seem extreme, and even fantastical; but it has its weight in explaining why—at the outset, at least—we held our ground. In the long discussion which followed, that night, it was evident that each party was urgent that the other should suggest abandonment of the premises. Neither, however, would broach the subject, and we separated for bed at last with the implied understanding that we were to remain.

CHAPTER VII

A GHOSTLY CO-TENANCY

Such was the first manifestation of a Possession which held the house for more than nine months. That we endured it is to me now sufficient cause for wonder, and the reasons why we did so (reasons which presented themselves by degrees) may require some explanation. It must be said that with the exception of a few visitations which I shall duly describe, there were no occasions so terrifying as those which happened on the day of the storm. Moreover, as my wife and I had made acquaintance in former years with many inexplicable things and had never seen any serious results come from them, our attitude toward these new phenomena was one compact more of curiosity than anything else. The experience could hardly be called agreeable, but it was strange and unusual, and we wanted to find out what it all meant. We never *did* find out, by the way, but the anticipation (which was constant) that we should, kept us interested.

The amiable reader may be disposed to credit us with unusual courage, but we never looked at the matter in that light. Besides the influence of national pride which I have mentioned as supporting both our friend and ourselves, there was also the consideration that we had covenanted for the house for a year, and had paid the first six-months' rent in advance—and Yankee and Scottish thrift alike moved us to desire our money's worth; and although we might hope to annul our bargain if we could plead that the dwelling was infested with rats, we had doubts as to our standing in court in case we should set up a defense that it was overrun with ghosts. Moreover, we liked our quarters so well that we could not make up our minds to leave them merely because an unseen co-tenantry insisted on sharing them with us; therefore we remained, and in time even managed to extract some entertainment from the quips and cranks that were more or less constantly going on.

A saving feature of the situation was the fact that the manifestations were not continuous, and rarely occurred—until near the end of our term—at night. This, I think, must be set down as an unusual circumstance, but it was one that brought us considerable relief. It need not be pointed out, for example, how much less terrifying it is to hear muffled footsteps and the rustle of women's garments up and down the hall by daylight than in darkness, and to see, under the same conditions, chairs and light tables shifted about in apparent accordance with some invisible person's notion of their proper arrangement. It is somewhat disquieting, to be sure, when walking through the hall, to hear the bell above one's head break out in rattling clangor, and, looking through the wide-open front door, to perceive that no visible visitor was at the other end of the wire:—and in spite of many former experiences, we could not restrain ourselves from jumping in our seats when, at dinner, all the doors in the house would slam in rapid succession with a violence that set the dishes dancing on the board. And the singular thing about this performance was that although the sound was unmistakably that of banging doors, the doors themselves seemed to have no part in it. More than once we arranged them in anticipation of this manifestation, leaving some closed, some wide open, and some ajar at various angles which we carefully noted. Presently would come the expected thunderous reverberations—and running from the dining-room we would find every door precisely as we had left it.

Occasionally, what seemed like a rushing

wind would sweep through the hall between the wire-screened doors at either end of the house, although a glance out of the window showed that the leaves of the trees in the yard were pendent and lifeless in an utter calm:—and this circumstance reminds me of a curious thing that was several times repeated.

We rarely used the parlor, which, as I have said, was on the right of the hall as one entered the house, with windows giving upon the veranda. To the decorations of this room which had been left by our landlord, we had made some considerable additions—photographs of New Zealand scenery, curios and wall hangings from Fiji, and other such matters. Now and then would break out in that room a racket as though a dozen devils were dancing the tarantelle, accompanied by a sound as of a maëlstrom of wind whirling in it. We never had courage to enter while the disturbance was in progress—in fact we had no time to do so, as it always ended within a few minutes; but when we opened the door after the noise had subsided, we invariably found the same condition of affairs—every article in the room that belonged to *us* piled in a heap on the floor, and all the possessions of the absent family standing or hanging undisturbed in their usual places. We were disposed to regard this demonstration as a gentle hint that our continuation in the house was not desired, and that the "spooks," as we came familiarly to call them, had in furtherance of this idea gathered together such of our belongings as they could reach in order to facilitate our packing up for departure. But we paid no heed to the implied suggestion, restored the room to its former condition, and in a short time this particular form of annoyance was discontinued.

These were minor occurrences, and I am not relating them with any reference to the order in which they came. As they seem to belong to the general run of phenomena that have been frequently noticed in accounts of "haunted houses"—so called—I will not dwell upon them; merely observing that the effort to produce them was entirely misplaced if its purpose was to frighten us, and in any case unworthy of any intelligent source. I more than once announced this opinion in a loud tone of voice when the rustlings and footfalls, and their often accompanying groans and sighs became too persistent, or wearisome in their lack of variety—and it was curious to see how effective this remonstrance always was. A dead silence would immediately ensue, and for hours, and sometimes even for days, the house would be as orderly and commonplace as possible.

It is my recollection that the mother of Deeming (if, indeed, she it were) made no further appearance after her son's execution. She seems to have expressed herself in one supreme and futile appeal for help, and then to have gone to her place. Several others followed her, whom I could hear from time to time as they moved about, and whom my wife, whose clearness of sight in these matters I never shared, described as an old woman, another much younger, and a girl-child some four or five years of age. They never attempted any communication with us; in fact, they seemed quite unaware of our presence; and were evidently not concerned in any of the bizarre and seemingly meaningless manifestations that were continually going on. We fancied that the shade of the elder woman was that of the former mistress of the house, whose death, as I have already noted, had occurred therein some three months before we took possession:—but as she ignored us entirely, we respected her seeming disinclination to a mutual introduction, and left her to go to and fro in the way she preferred. This way was not altogether a pleasant one. She wore a black gown, my wife musical, for all that. On rarer occasions she would sing to herself a song, but one in which no words could be distinguished; in all her utterances, indeed, there was never anything that sounded like speech. She was not quite sure of herself in this song. Now and then she would strike a wrong note; then silence for a moment, and she would begin the song again. As she reached the note at which she had before stumbled, she would pause, then take the note correctly, give a pleased little laugh, and go on successfully to the end.

This extraordinary performance was repeated on many occasions. One bright Sunday afternoon I was sitting in talk with my wife in her room, when this weird chant started up in the farthest corner. I listened through the whole of the usual rendition—the beginning, the false note, the return for a new trial, the note rightly struck, the satisfied laugh, and so on to the conclusion. Then the thing began all over again.

I said, rather impatiently: "Don't sing that again! Can't you see that we want to talk?"

"Oh, you shouldn't have said that!" remonstrated my wife. "She has gone away"—and in fact the song had stopped, and it was many days before we heard it again.

said, with a neckerchief of some white material—the rustle of her gown, which I could plainly hear, indicated that it was of silk; she seemed unhappy (we thought it might be that she did not understand the absence of her husband and daughters) and was forever sighing softly and wringing her hands. The younger woman (the two never seemed to be conscious of each others' existence—if that is the right word) was in a state of evident discomfort also, although she was always silent, and appeared to be constantly in search of something she could not find.

Altogether we found these shadowy guests of ours a rather cheerless company; but as we had had no voice in inviting them, and feared that their departure (if they should accept any intimation from us that it was desired) might make room for others even more objectionable, we were fain to adapt ourselves to the situation that was forced upon us. The child-ghost, however, was of quite different disposition. She had something with her that seemed to take the place of a doll, and would sit with it by the hour in a corner of the room where we all were, at times crooning to it in a queer, far-away, but still quite audible voice. It was a "creepy" thing to hear, but strangely sweet and

THE HAUNTED BUNGALOW

I have not particularly mentioned our friend in this recital of minor happenings, although he had his share in most of them, and carried himself throughout in a plucky and admirable manner. We were very fond of him, as he evidently was of us to endure adventures with us which he must have found uncongenial, to say the least—he being a man of quiet tastes, and one not prone to go out of his way in search for excitement. An incident that happened one night, however, came very near to ending his residence with us.

At about eight o'clock of an evening in June (the time of year when the days are at their shortest in that latitude), he and I were smoking and chatting in my "den," my wife being in her own room at the front of the house. All at once the two dogs who were chained in the back yard broke out in a terrific chorus of barking. They were ordinarily very quiet animals, and whenever they gave tongue (which was only when some tradesman or other person came upon the premises by the back gate) it was merely by a yelp or two to inform us that they were attending to their duty as guardians. On this occasion, however, one might have thought there were a dozen dogs behind the house instead of two:—they seemed fairly frantic, and there was a strange note in their voices such as I had never heard before.

"What on earth is the matter with those dogs?" I exclaimed. "One might think they were being murdered."

"They are certainly tremendously excited about something," my companion rejoined:—"let's go out and see what the trouble is"—and he was out of the room, and unlocking the back door, before I could leave my easy-chair to accompany him. As I reached the hall I was just in time to see the large pane of groundglass with which the upper half of the outside door was fitted, fly inward—shattered into a thousand pieces by a jagged fragment of rock as large as my fist, which whizzed by my friend's head with such force that it went by me also, and brought up against the front door at the other end of the hall. My companion, who had escaped death or a serious injury by the smallest possible margin, fell back against the wall with his hands over his face, which had been cut in several places by the flying glass; but he quickly recovered himself, and when I had hastened back to my room and provided myself with a revolver, we rushed together into the open air. Nothing was to be seen, nor could we hear a sound. We went into the street, which was lighted by scattered gas lamps, and listened for retreating footsteps, but the street was vacant as far as we could see in both directions, and the silence of the night was like that of the grave. We dragged the dogs out of the kennels to which they had retreated, and turned them loose in the hope that their peculiar intelligence would enable them to guide us to some lurking miscreant in the shrubbery about the yard or amid the trees and vines in the obscurity of the orchard:—but they were trembling as if in abject fear, we could get no help from them, and when released they bolted into their kennels again and hid themselves in the straw at the farthest corners. It was evident that they had seen something that terrified them greatly, but what it was we could only surmise. The Scotch terrier was a gentle creature, and his evident alarm did not so much surprise me. The fox-terrier, on the other hand, was full of "bounce" and confidence, and nothing in canine or human shape had any terrors for him. When it came to devils, that might be another matter—an idea that passed through my mind at the time, but did not then find lodgment. It was strengthened in view of another incident which occurred later, and which I shall describe in a subsequent chapter.

CHAPTER VIII

THE DEAD WALKS

THE incident of the flying stone and the broken glass much disquieted us, and furnished matter of anxious discussion for several days. It gave us the first hint we had received that the influences that seemed to be busy about us included any of a malign or violent nature, and inspired a lively apprehension of other sinister happenings of which it might be the forerunner. There was, of course, the doubt as to whether the affair might not be due to human agency; had it stood by itself, no other idea would have occurred to us:—but although we tried to satisfy ourselves that some reckless or malicious person was the culprit, the attendant circumstances seemed to point away from that opinion. The force with which the missile was hurled indicated that no mischievous boy could have aimed it, while it appeared incredible that any man would take the risk of passing the clamorous dogs and crossing the wide yard to take a point-blank shot at the door—as the direct course of the stone showed had been done.

Nor could it have been thrown from any considerable distance:—the laundry outhouse before mentioned, was not more than thirty feet from the door and protected it from any attack outside that limit. It was the behavior of the dogs, however, that puzzled us the most. Instead of welcoming our coming, as would naturally have been the case, they shrunk from the touch of our hands and gave no heed to our voices, but shook and shivered as if in an ague fit.

In spite of these facts, the event so much smacked of the material, and was so opposed in its nature to anything else that had happened, that we hesitated to attribute it to the agency of unseen powers; and as the week that followed was free of any alarming incident we decided to keep it out of the debit column of our account with the "spooks," and give them the credit of having had no part in it.

It was, I think (although I am uncertain about the exact date) about a fortnight after the stone-throwing episode, that I came home one afternoon much earlier than usual; and as my wife met me at the door I saw at once that look upon her face which had on several occasions advised me that something quite out of the ordinary had happened during my absence. It is hardly necessary for me to mention, in view of the record already made of the experience she had shared with me in that ill-omened house, that among her notable characteristics were high courage and self-control. On this occasion, however, her appearance alarmed me greatly. There was a presence of fear upon her; she was *distraite* and nervous, despite her evident effort to appear unconcerned; and the strange expression which I had often seen when her gaze seemed to follow the movements of shapes invisible to my grosser sense, still clouded her eyes.

I did not at once question her, although I was consumed with curiosity, and tried to quiet her evident, although suppressed, excitement by talking of the commonplace incidents of my day in town. But it was apparent that she did not hear a word I said:—indeed, her attitude and manner were as of one who listened to another voice than mine; and I soon lapsed into silence and sat watching her with a growing anxiety.

Suddenly the obsession with which she seemed to be contending passed away:—she turned impulsively to me and cried:

"We must leave this house! I have endured

all I can! I will not remain here another day!"

"I knew that something was wrong the moment I saw you," I said. "Something very bad has happened—do you want to tell me what it is?"

"Oh, I cannot, I cannot!" she exclaimed. "It is too horrible; it would frighten you to death if I should tell you!"

"Anything that you have gone through, I ought to be able to hear of," I replied. "I think you had better tell me your story, and get it off your mind, before our friend comes home."

"Oh, he must never know it!" she cried. "Promise me that you will not tell him!"

"Of course I will not tell him, if you do not wish it," I assented. "And now let me know what has alarmed you."

During our conversation I had imagined all sorts of terrifying incidents as having occurred —but my wife's next words sent a shiver through me.

"Deeming has been here," she said.

"Deeming!" I exclaimed; "that devil!"

"Yes," she replied. "He did not try to harm me, but if there is a Hell he came from it. Oh, he is so wretched and unhappy! In spite of the horror of seeing him, I was never so sorry for any creature in all my life. Just to look at him was enough to make me know what is meant by 'the torments of the damned'—such awful suffering! I shall never get his sad and frightful face out of my mind!"—and she covered her face with her hands, as if still seeing the terrific vision that she had described.

When she had partially recovered her composure, she began at the beginning and told me the whole story. It so impressed me that, even at this distance of time, I remember perfectly every detail of the narration, and almost its every word, and with this recollection I set it down.

"It was about an hour before you came home," she began, and I was sewing at the front window of my room, when I heard the latch of the gate click. I looked up, and saw that someone was coming into the yard. It was a man—a peddler, I thought—and I went to the door to tell him that I did not wish to buy anything. The door was open, although the outside screen door was shut and bolted. I had no idea at all that it was not a living human being; but when I got to the door and looked at the figure, which was standing just inside the gate and facing the house, I knew it was nothing that belonged to *this world*. It was misty and indistinct, and I could not make out any details of face or costume, except that the clothes seemed mean and cheap.

"I don't know how long I stood there," she continued, after a pause; "but by-and-by the Thing began to come toward me up the walk. It didn't seem exactly to walk—it just *moved*, I cannot tell you how; and as it got nearer, although I couldn't distinguish the features, I began to see the clothes quite clearly."

"What were the clothes like?" I here interrupted.

"They were the strangest-looking things I ever saw on anybody," she replied. "There was no style or fit to them, and they seemed more like clothes made of flour sacks than anything else—very coarse and ungainly. And an odd thing about them was that they had queer triangular black designs on them here and there. But the cap the figure wore was the strangest thing of all:—it was of dingy white cloth and fitted close to the head, and it had a sort of flap hanging down behind almost to the shoulders:—what did you say?"—for I had uttered a sudden ejaculation.

"Nothing," I replied:—"please go on."

"Well," she continued, "the figure came up to the two steps leading to the veranda, and I think it would have come up to the door; but I said, 'Stop!' and it stood still where it was. It was still indistinct, and I felt as though it strained my eyes to see it; the face was vague, and did not seem like any face I had ever seen before.

"I said: 'Who are you, and what do you want?'

"The Thing held out something it had in its hand, but I couldn't make out what it was, and made the strangest reply. It said: 'Madame, do you want to buy some soap?'"

"Gracious powers!" I exclaimed:—"It was Deeming?—and he asked you to buy *soap?*"

"I did not know it was Deeming until later," replied my wife; "but I have told you what he said in his exact words. What could he mean by offering to sell me soap?"

"I have an idea about that which I will tell you of presently. But first let me hear the rest of the story."

"Well," she went on, "I told him I did not want any soap. 'But,' he said, 'I must sell some, and I beg of you to buy it'—and when I again refused, his voice took on the saddest, most pathetic tone, and he said: 'I thought you would. You were kinder to me when you saw me in the jail.' 'I never saw you before in my life!' I said—for truly I did not recognize him even then; but he said: 'Oh, yes, you have, and you tried to get Miss Rounsfell to come and see me.' 'What!' I cried; 'are you Deeming?'—and he said: 'Yes, madame, I am that unfortunate man.'

"I don't quite know what I said after that. I felt as though I should die of fright, and I think I screamed to him to go away, that the thought of his dreadful crimes horrified me so that I could not look at him, and that he must never come to me again. He looked at me reproachfully and turned away. I watched him go to the gate, open it as anyone might have done, and close it after him—then he vanished instantly, the moment he had got into the street. But I know he'll be back! He is suffering, and I am the only one he can reach. I don't know what he wants, but I cannot see him again. It will kill me or drive me mad if we stay here!"

I certainly felt that I had parted with my own wits by the time this astounding tale was concluded. It was so awful in its facts and in its suggestions, its details combined in such a mixture of the hideous and the grotesque, that I looked anxiously at my wife in the fear that what I personally knew to have taken place in the house had upset her mind, and produced this dreadful hallucination. But how to attribute to hallucination certain items in the story which referred to facts with which *I* was acquainted, but of which she was ignorant until her experience of the afternoon had revealed them to her?

At her express desire I had told her nothing of the execution which I had witnessed, and she had strictly refrained from reading about it in the newspapers:—yet she had described accurately, and in all its details, the garb he wore on the scaffold—the uncouth trousers and jacket of sacking, stamped with the "Broad Arrow" that marked both it and its wearer to be the property of the Crown, and the ghastly "death cap," with its pendent flap behind which was pulled forward and dropped over his face just before the trap was sprung!

And the *soap!*—that, as I explained to her, seemed the most gruesome feature of all. My theory regarding it may have been fanciful:—yet what was this poor bedeviled ghost more likely to have with him than a sample of the material that had been used upon the rope that hung him, to make it smooth and pliant, and swift of action in the noose?

But why had he wished to sell it, and what help could he hope to gain thereby? He had evidently come, not to frighten, but to crave relief from some distressed condition, and when he failed to gain it he had gone away disappointed, but in sorrow rather than in anger.

When morning came, after a night of which we spent the greater part in discussion of this new and disconcerting development, my wife surprised me by saying that she had changed her mind about leaving the house, and had decided to remain. I strongly remonstrated against her exposing herself to a more than possible danger, but she continued firm in her resolution—said she was convinced that the apparition had no purpose to harm or even alarm her, and that it might be her duty, as it would certainly be her effort, if it came again, to ascertain the cause of its disquiet, and, if possible, remove it.

This decision caused me great uneasiness for several days:—but as the spectre did not return I began to think that its first visit was also its last, and began to interest myself anew in the cantrips with which the house goblins continued to amuse themselves and mystify us.

CHAPTER IX

THE GOBLINS OF THE KITCHEN

AMONG the things that impressed us amid the general goings-on about the house was the evidence of a certain sort of humor in the make-up of the influences that were seemingly responsible for them. That this humor did not particularly appeal to our taste, I must admit; it seemed distinctly lacking in subtlety, and suggested that its authors might be the spirits of certain disembodied low comedians of the bladder-and-slapstick variety. To some such agency, at least, we came to attribute the phenomena of the slamming doors, jingling door bell, and occasional upsetting of the parlor; and from time to time other things occurred to break this monotony of elfish sprightliness, and to show us that our spookish friends were not mere creatures of routine, but were full of waggish resource. The indoor incidents that I have already narrated may seem to have borne the ancient ghostly—or "poltergeistic"—trademark, and to have been contrived and employed after a conventional and long-approved plan:

—but if there is anywhere a Shadowland Patent Office, the originators of the pranks I am about to describe should be enjoying its protection for their ingenious inventions.

I was sitting in my room at about noon, one day, awaiting a call to the luncheon which my wife was preparing. Suddenly I heard her call out from the front hall: "Come here, quick! I have something queer to show you!" I went out at once, and found her standing at the door of the dark chamber I have previously described, wherein we were accustomed to keep milk, butter, and other such provisions, for the sake of coolness.

"Look in there," said my wife—and I looked in accordingly; but I observed nothing unusual, and so reported.

"Look up," she said again. I did so, and saw a large milk pan resting motionless in the air just under the ceiling several feet above my head and just beneath the perforated opening of the ventilator. I naturally inquired how it had got there.

"I hardly know," replied my wife; "the thing was done so quickly. The pan is full of milk, and was resting on the floor of the hollow space when I came to get some of the milk for our lunch. I had taken up the pan, when it was snatched from my hands and floated up to the place where you now see it."

"This is something new," I remarked, "and rather interesting. I hope the spooks are not drinking the milk"—and as I spoke, the pan began deliberately to descend. When it was within reach I caught hold of the handle on each side, and tried to accelerate its motion. It stopped immediately, and although I employed considerable force I could not budge it. (The effect was not at all as if I were pulling against a physical force like my own; the pan was as immovable and inert as though it were a component part of the masonry of the chamber about it.) I stood aside, therefore; whereupon it began to float down again, and shortly settled in its former place on the floor, touching it so lightly that the contact did not cause even a ripple upon the surface of the milk. We tasted that milk very carefully before venturing to use it for our repast, but found nothing wrong with it.

A few evenings after the episode of the levitating milk pan, we all three went into Melbourne after dinner to attend the theatre. After the performance and while on the way to our train we passed a cook-shop, in whose window was displayed a quantity of roasted duck and teal, the game season then being at its height. They looked so appetizing that I was moved to go in and purchase a pair of teal for a shilling or two (these birds were astonishingly plentiful, and correspondingly cheap in Australia at the time), had them put into a paper box, and carried them home with the view to a light supper before we should go to bed. As it seemed hardly worth while to use the dining-room, we went into the kitchen; where I put the teal on a platter and prepared to carve them while my wife was arranging the plates and necessary cutlery. The carving knife was in its usual place in the knife-box, but I could not find the fork that went with it, and so remarked.

"Why," said my wife, "it's there with the knife, of course." She spoke with conviction and authority, for among her conspicuous traits was a love for orderliness in all things pertaining to the household.

Nevertheless, the fork was *not* there; nor could we find it, although we overhauled everything in the cupboard in search for it. Meanwhile our friend, actuated by the laudable purpose of keeping out of the way of our preparations, was standing near the door, with his hands in his pockets.

"I see it!" he suddenly exclaimed, and withdrawing one hand from its confinement, he pointed upward. My eye followed the direction thus indicated, and I also saw the missing utensil:—it was stuck into the upper part of the window casing, just under the ceiling, and a folded paper was impaled upon its tines. I got upon the table and took the fork from its position. It required considerable force to do so, for the tines were deeply imbedded in the woodwork. Then I unfolded the paper. It was about four inches square, and drawn upon it, with much spirit and a strict adherence to the principles of realism in art, were a skull and crossbones. These were done in a red medium which at first we thought was blood, but which we finally decided to be ink, since it retained its color for weeks, and did not darken, as blood would have done. There was no writing whatever on the sheet; therefore we had no reason to regard it as an attention from the "Black Hand"—another reason being that we had never heard of the "Black Hand" at that time. We had no red ink in the house, nor any paper like that upon which the design was drawn—and nothing ever occurred to throw any light on the matter.

This incident—like that of the hurled stone

—seemed so palpably referable to human agency that it revived the rather feeble hope we had from time to time entertained that we might, after all, be the victims of some ingenious trickery. Therefore our friend and I devoted one afternoon to a close search of the house, outhouse, and the premises generally, particularly exploring the dusty attic for concealed machinery—in short, for anything that might give a clue to the mystery. We emerged from the attic looking like a couple of sweeps, but this was the only result achieved; nor did we accomplish anything else in all our investigations. As for the attic, nobody could get into it otherwise than by bringing the ladder into the house from the outhouse and raising it to the trap-door in the ceiling of the bathroom. As to outside origin of the various pranks that had been played upon us, we could see no way in which they could be performed in view of the fact that we had every facility to observe the approach of any mischief-maker:—since we had a wide street on two sides of us, and the houses on each of the other two sides were at least a hundred yards away. The fact that most of the "manifestations" with which we had been favored had occurred in the daytime added to the puzzle; the only two things that we could explain as perhaps the work of beings like ourselves (the episodes of the thrown stone and of the fork) had occurred under the cover of darkness:—therefore, hoping that, with these data to go upon, we might get to the cause of our annoyances, we set a trap with the hope that if any practical joker were at work, he might walk into it.

In furtherance of this purpose I sent my wife and our friend to the theatre, a few evenings later, accompanying them to the railway station after extinguishing all the lights in the house in order to create the impression in the mind of any possible watcher of our movements that we were all three equally on pleasure bent in town, and returning by a devious route which finally brought me by a scramble over the orchard fence to the back door. I quietly let myself into the house, arranged an easy chair at a point where I could command the hall in both directions, and sat down amid utter darkness, with my revolver in my jacket pocket and my shot gun, heavily charged in both barrels, across my knees. I was fully determined to test the materiality—or otherwise—of any shape that might present itself, by turning my artillery loose thereon without any preliminary word of challenge; but although my vigil lasted until midnight, I was obliged to report to my returning companions that nothing whatever had happened.

I may add that that evening was the longest and least agreeable I ever experienced.

It may be that the incident with which I shall close this rather rambling chapter was promoted by the same humorists who devised the conceit of the floating milk pan, and was employed as a means of enabling us to recognize therein the authors of the former whimsicality. The two pleasantries seemed, at all events, to have been conceived in the same spirit, and although both were equally odd and purposeless, the superior elaborateness of the second distinctly showed an advance over the first, and gained our applause accordingly. There was no connection between these episodes in point of time; in fact, the second occurred several months after the first, in the hottest part of the year.

Our friend being a Briton by birth and an Australian by adoption, he had enjoyed rather a narrow experience in dietetics, particularly in the vegetable line. During the early part of our housekeeping we had found much difficulty in securing for our table any garden delicacies outside the conventional list of potatoes, "vegetable marrow," and cauliflower—until Providence brought to our back door an amiable Chinese huckster, who, with several compatriots, had established a small truck-farm in the neighborhood. Earnest representations regarding our vegetableless conditions inspired his interest, and the promise of good prices awakened his cupidity; and as a result of the agreement of these motives it was not long before our table greatly improved.

And I cannot help saying—although this is a digression—that our often-expressed words of satisfaction to our purveyor stimulated him to produce and bring to us everything of the best that he could raise. In his way he was an artist, with an artist's craving for praise—so that now and then he would appear with a gift of some new product for us to try, and occasionally with a small packet of choice tea or some other Celestial delicacy, for which he would invariably refuse payment.

"You should not bring me these things," my wife said to him one day. "You can't afford them."

"Me likee bling 'em," he replied. "An' me likee *you*. You no ploud. Mos' lady too ploud"—and swinging his baskets to his shoulder he departed.

It was my wife's delight to tempt our friend's appetite with all sorts of culinary novelties, which the new and more liberal order of things allowed her to prepare. With true British conservatism he would venture gingerly upon an unfamiliar dish, admit it "wasn't half bad," and end by eating as much of it as both of us others together. It was finally discovered that a particularly effective way of appeal to his nature was through the medium of baked stuffed tomatoes:—of these he seemed never to have enough, and, as a consequence, they were frequently upon our bill-of-fare during the summer. It seems incredible—and lamentable—that a man should have got well into the fifties without ever having eaten a baked stuffed tomato:—such, however, was our friend's unhappy case, and my wife made strenuous efforts to ameliorate it.

"I have a treat for you to-night," she said to our friend. "Guess what it is."

"Baked stuffed tomatoes," he responded promptly—and baked stuffed tomatoes it was.

"Now," continued my wife, "you two men must eat your dinner in the kitchen to-night. The woman who cooks for me is ill to-day, and you will have to take pot-luck. I have let the fire in the stove go out, and have been using the gas range; so you will find the kitchen cooler than the dining-room, and by eating there you will save me work, besides."

So we went into the kitchen, where we found the table already laid for us.

"Before we sit down," said my wife, turning smilingly to our friend, "I am going to show you the treat you were so clever in guessing. But you are not to have it at once; that will come after the cold meat. The tomatoes are nice and hot, and I have put them in here to keep them from cooling too fast:"—and with these words she kneeled upon the floor and opened the iron door which shut in a wide but shallow cavity in the masonry that formed the base of the open fireplace.

This fireplace was an unusual feature in a modern kitchen, and we, at least, had never put it to any use. It projected slightly into the room, and on the sides of it, and against the wall in each case, were, respectively, the cook stove and gas range. Under its hearth, and but a few inches above the level of the room, was the hollow space I have mentioned—I believe it was what is sometimes called a "Dutch oven"—eight inches high, perhaps, two feet wide, and eighteen inches deep. From this space my wife partly drew out for our inspection an iron baking pan, in which an even dozen of deliciously cooked, golden-and-red, crumb-stuffed tomatoes were sociably shouldering each other:—then, after hearing our expressions of satisfaction with their appearance, she pushed the pan back again, closed the iron door, and sat down with us to dinner.

The table stood against the wall, directly under the window. My wife was seated at the end next to the fireplace, I was opposite her, and our friend was at the side, his back to the hall door and his face to the window. Thus he and my wife were each within two feet of the fireplace and the chamber under it, and the iron door guarding our treasure was in direct range of my own eyes from the position I occupied.

Having despatched the earlier portions of the repast, my wife arose, removed the used dishes to a side table, set others in their places, and with the remark: "Now for the tomatoes!" swung open the iron door under the fireplace. The interior, however, was absolutely empty:—the tomatoes, and the heavy baking pan that had held them, had disappeared!

Our friend and I sprang from our chairs in astonishment and incredulity—but the fact was undoubted; the treat which had been so much anticipated had been snatched, as it were, from our very lips. Our friend turned from one to the other of us a face so comically set between wonder and disappointment that I burst out laughing in spite of myself. But my ill-timed levity was promptly checked by my wife, who was at the moment giving a competent imitation of a lioness robbed of her whelps.

"Oh!" she cried, seemingly addressing nothing in particular, although she might have felt —as I did—that she was speaking to a derisive audience; "that is too bad of you! To steal my tomatoes, when I worked over them so long! Bring them back instantly!" But they remained invisible, and over all a sarcastic silence brooded. Then she turned upon us unfortunate men.

"Have you been playing me a trick?" she demanded. "Do *you* know what has become of those tomatoes?"—"Certainly not"—this to both questions. Neither of us had moved from his chair since we sat down to dinner and she had shown us the pan and its contents. Nor had she, for that matter, except when she had risen to change the dishes, and even then she had not left the room.

All that could be said was that the tomatoes had been exhibited, and then had been shut up again behind the door. There was no possible doubt about that—it was equally certain that they had vanished. Very well, then let us search for them! This we did, and with great thoroughness, all over the house, and in every part of the grounds; the outhouse at the back was also carefully inspected. I even got the ladder and went, in turn, upon the roofs of both structures, looked down the chimneys:— "nothing doing" (to employ an Oriental expression not then, unhappily, in use); nowhere any trace of the missing pan or of the tomatoes.

We gave it up finally, and went back to our dessert and coffee. My wife refused to be satisfied that the tomatoes were actually gone. She was constantly getting up to open the iron door and view the emptiness behind it—as if she expected the apparent dematerialization of the pan and tomatoes to be reversed,—while our friend looked on with an aspect of forced resignation.

I left them after a time, and went out for an after-dinner smoke on the back doorstep. I had hardly lighted my pipe when I heard a cry blended of two voices in the kitchen—a shriek from my wife, and a mildly profane ejaculation from our friend. Rushing in, I saw an astonishing sight—our friend, with staring eyes and blanched face, supporting himself against the table as if staggered by a blow, my wife kneeling in front of the open iron door beneath the fireplace, and the baking pan and its dozen tomatoes lying before her on the floor!

It was some time before I could get a coherent account of what had happened. It was finally developed, however, that after I had left the room the conversation continued on the inexplicable conduct of the tomatoes. "I can't believe they are not there!" my wife asserted, and, for the dozenth time or so, she again knelt on the floor and again opened the door.

"I was standing right behind her," said our friend, "and saw her swing the door open, but there was nothing inside. At the same instant I heard a thump on the floor, and there the whole outfit was, just in front of her. I don't know where the things came from—perhaps down the chimney:—at any rate, one moment there was nothing there; the next, the pan and the tomatoes were on the floor."

After we had regained our composure we considered what we should do with the tomatoes. Our friend said he didn't think *he* wanted any of them, and I confessed to an equal indifference—so capricious, and often influenced by slight circumstances, is the appetite!

My wife, as usual, settled the matter. "Take them away!" she said. "Throw them into the garbage barrel!"—which was accordingly done; melancholy end of a culinary triumph! Yet we ought at least to have tasted those tomatoes: under the title *"tomato à la diable"* they might have found a place in the cook books.

CHAPTER X

A SPECTRAL BURGLARY

I CANNOT but consider it an interesting circumstance that the varied happenings in the House on the Hill seemed to arrange themselves into two rather strictly defined classes —the sportive and the terrible—and that the respective influences responsible for them appeared carefully to refrain from interfering with each others' functions or prerogatives. As among our earthly acquaintances we number some who are entirely deficient in appreciation of the ridiculous, and others so flippant as to have no sense of the serious, so, it seemed to us, the unseen friends who so diversely made their presence known were in like manner to be differentiated.

In this connection another singular fact is to be noted. While the clownish performers in the juggling of the milk pan, the prestidigitation of the baked stuffed tomatoes, and other such specialties, always remained invisible, even to my wife, what I may call the more dramatic manifestations were accompanied by apparitions that were the evident actors in them. It also occurred to us that if the "acts" that were staged for our benefit were to be regarded as presenting what passed for entertainment in the Dark World, there must be drawn there, as here, a sharp line of distinction between vaudeville and "the legitimate;" incidentally, too, it would seem that ghostly audiences were like many in the flesh in their capacity for being easily entertained.

However that may be, we somehow came to the opinion that while the more impressive of the phenomena with which we were favored appeared to be due to the action of beings that had aforetime been upon the earth—for in every such case the attending spectres were to be identified as *simulacra* of persons whose previous existence was known to some one (and generally all) of us,—the tricksy antics that seemed to come from Nowhere might find their impulse in elementary entities or forces which had not yet exercised their activities upon the earth plane (and, indeed, might never be intended to do so), and thus had never assumed a material form. I do not put this forward as a theory, but simply as a passing impression that lightly brushed our minds:—and to repel the temptation of being led into the seductive regions of speculation, I will re-assume my *rôle* as a mere narrator of facts and describe a quite inexplicable affair that occurred near the close of our tenancy.

The bedroom which I have before described as being at the front of the house, with two windows overlooking the veranda, was occupied at night by my wife and myself. Between the windows was a ponderous mahogany dressing table, surmounted by a large mirror. This article of furniture was so broad that it extended on either side beyond the inner casing of the windows, and so heavy that it required the united strength of both of us to move it—as, during the cleaning of the room, we sometimes had to do. The windows were protected by wire screens, secured by stout bolts which were shot into sockets in the woodwork, and fitted flush with the surface of the outer window casing. In February—the time of which I am writing—the weather was at its hottest, and we slept at night with the windows open, trusting our security to the strong wire screens.

One morning, after an untroubled night's sleep, I awoke soon after sunrise, and from my

THE HAUNTED BUNGALOW

place in bed, nearest the window, looked lazily out upon the day. Still half-asleep, I lay for some time without noting anything unusual; but as my sensibilities revived I observed that the screen was missing from the left-hand window, and that the dressing table, instead of standing in its usual place against the wall, was turned half-way around, and projected at right angles into the room. I was out of bed in an instant, and at the window—looking out of which I saw the screen lying flat on the floor of the veranda. I went out and examined it. It was uninjured, and the bolts still projected from either side to show that they had not been drawn; but two deep grooves in the woodwork of the casing indicated that the screen had been dragged outward from its place. How this damage could have been done to the stout casing, without marring in the least the comparatively light frame of the screen, I could by no means understand—particularly as there was no possible way by which one could get a hold upon the outside of the screen except by the use of screws or gimlets to act as holds for one's hands; and of these there were no marks whatever.

I had made this examination so quietly that I had not awakened my wife:—now, however,

I returned to the bedroom and aroused her.

Her first thought, on seeing the condition of affairs, was that burglars had visited us:—my idea had been the same until I had observed the peculiar facts that I have just noted. Tacitly accepting this theory for the moment, I assisted her in making an inventory of our portable valuables. While I satisfied myself that my purse and watch were safe, my wife took her keys from under the pillow (where she always kept them at night) and went to the dressing table, in one of whose drawers was her jewel box. The drawer was locked, and so was the jewel box, and the latter, on being opened, seemed to hold all its usual contents intact.

"No," she said, after mentally checking off the various articles; "everything is here; nothing has been taken. Wait! I am wrong; one thing is missing. Do you remember that rhinestone brooch in the shape of a butterfly you bought for me one evening in Paris, four years ago?"

"Why, yes," I replied; "I got it in a shop under the arcades on the Rue de Rivoli, and paid five francs for it. You don't mean to say that the thieves, or our friends the 'spooks,' or whoever it may be, have taken that trifle and left your diamond rings and other things really valuable untouched!"

Yet such appeared to be the case—the cheap and unimportant brooch was the only thing unaccounted for, nor had anything else been disturbed throughout the house. It seemed incredible that any burglar who had passed merely the kindergarten stage of schooling in his profession could have been deceived into supposing that this commonplace *article de Paris* had any value; besides, why should *this* have been taken and the real jewelry that lay with it in the same box have been left? And how had it been extracted from the locked box inside the locked dressing table? The keys of both were on the same ring under my wife's pillow, and although a robber might extract them without awaking her, it seemed unreasonable to suppose he would take the additional risk of replacing them when he had completed his work. But for these and other questions that presented themselves we could find no satisfactory answers.

We ate our breakfast in a state of mild expectation that the brooch might be returned as mysteriously as it had been taken. The adventure seemed to be constructed on lines similar to those laid down in the affair of the baked stuffed tomatoes, and we were disposed to credit it to the same agency;—but if the sprites who were responsible for the former prank had contrived this later one also, they either intended to carry it no further, or were preparing a different *dénouement*. This last conjecture proved to be the true one, but we had to wait a long time for the fact to be developed.

We gave our "spooks" sufficient time to consummate their joke (if, indeed, they were responsible for it), and finally concluding that they were not inclined to embrace the opportunity, we again took under consideration the burglar theory, and I went to the local police station to report the occurrence. Two heavyweight constables returned with me to the house and gravely inspected the premises. Their verdict was speedy and unanimous:—"Housebreakers." There had been similar breakings-and-enterings in the town recently—therefore the facts were obvious. I showed them the drawer and jewel box, and described the singular and modest spoil of the supposed thieves; I also exhibited the unmarred frame of the screen and the scarred window casing, and asked them how they explained *that*. This puzzled them, but they fell back easily upon the obvious and practical. "Housebreakers," they repeated. 'We shall make a report"—and marched away as ponderously as they had come. I did not acquaint them with the goings-on in that house for a year past:—had I done so, my prompt apprehension as a suspicious character would doubtless have followed.

In July of the following year I went from Philadelphia, where I was then living, to spend a few days with my wife at Savin Rock (near New Haven, Connecticut), where I had rented a cottage for the summer. The morning after my arrival I was awakened by my wife, who had risen but the moment before, and who, as I opened my eyes, exclaimed excitedly: "Look! Look at what is on the bureau!" Following with my eyes the direction of her pointed finger, I saw upon the bureau the pin-cushion into which I had stuck my scarf pin the night before, beside which, and in the centre of the cushion, appeared the butterfly brooch which I had last previously seen in Australia, sixteen months before!

"Where did you find it?" I asked, forgetting for the moment, and in my half-awake condition, the incident in which it had figured as above described.

"I didn't find it," my wife replied; "it is less than a minute ago that I saw it. It was not on the pin cushion last night; how in the world did it come here?"—"And from where?"—thus I completed the question.

Neither of us had any reply to this:—so I merely advanced the suggestion that it was pleasant to think that our spookish friends had not altogether forgotten us, although on our part we had no desire to cultivate their better acquaintance. This expression of sentiment may have had its effect:—at any rate, with the return of the brooch came an end to the mystery of "The House on the Hill."

CHAPTER XI

"REST, REST, PERTURBÉD SPIRIT!"

I THINK it was because such lighter incidents as those that I have described in the two preceding chapters were freely introduced among more weighty happenings, and thus gave a certain measure of relief from them, that we managed to fill out our term in the House on the Hill. Absurd and impish as the general run of these performances was, there was still an element of what I may almost call intimacy in them—a sort of appeal, as it were, to look upon the whole thing as a joke; which, while they caused us amazement, brought us no real alarm. Much as has been attributed to the influence of fear, I believe curiosity to be the stronger passion; and few days passed without a fillip being given to our interest by some new absurdity, while events of graver suggestion were few and far between.

I need not say that the affair which had been most sinister and disquieting was the coming to my wife of the evident apparition of Deeming. This visitation had been so awful and unearthly that by tacit agreement we had not spoken of it since the afternoon of its occurrence:—yet I had never been able to get it out of my mind, and every day I spent in town was darkened by forebodings of what might happen at home before my return. Each night as I came in sight of the house I looked anxiously for the figure of my wife standing on the veranda to welcome me, and each night I drew a breath of relief as I saw in her serene and smiling face that my apprehensions had been vain; and so I came by degrees to dismiss my fears in the conviction that that uneasy spirit had been laid at last.

But this comforting assurance suddenly failed me, when, one evening about two weeks after the ghost's first coming, I read in my wife's eyes that it had appeared again. Yet, greatly to my relief, I saw no fear in them, but, rather, an expression of pity. Her manner was quiet and composed, but I was sure she had been weeping.

"Yes," she said, in reply to my anxious inquiries; "Deeming has been here, and I have been crying. Oh, that poor tortured, despairing soul!—he is in Hell, and one infinitely worse than that we were taught to believe in; a Hell where conscience never sleeps, and where he sees what he might have been—and now never can be! He frightened me terribly at first, but I know he tried not to do so, and now I am glad he came, for I believe I have helped him, although I cannot understand how. I feel weak and faint, for I have been under a great strain, but I shall be better now that you have come home—and I know, too, that I shall never see him again. Come into my room, and I will tell you all about it:"—and when I had done so, and had tried, with some success, to quiet the agitation that, in spite of her words, still possessed her, she told me the amazing story of her experience.

"It was about eleven o'clock this forenoon," she began, "and I was alone in the house—in the kitchen. I had been airing the house, and all the doors and windows were open, although the screens were in place. All at once I heard the back gate creak as it always does when it opens, and 'Schneider' and 'Tokio'" (such were the names of our two dogs) "who were loose in the yard, barking at somebody. I supposed it was the butcher or the grocery man and looked out the back door—and just then the dogs came tearing by with their tails between their legs, and disappeared around the corner of the house. The next instant I saw a man standing just inside the gate. He was not looking at me, but his eyes seemed to be following the flight of the dogs; then they turned to meet mine, and I saw that it was Deeming. I shut the back door instantly and locked it—then ran to the front door and fastened *that;* I wanted to close and bolt the windows, too, but did not dare do so, for I was afraid I might look out of any one of them and see him. I prayed to God that he might go away, but he did not. I stood in the hall and saw him move by outside the window of your room. By-and-by he passed the dining-room window on the other side of me as I stood there, having gone completely around the house. But he did not look in.

"I did not see anything more of him for some time, and I began to think that he had given up trying to communicate with me, and had gone away again. I finally went into the bedroom and peeped out into the veranda. He was there, standing near and facing the door! He did not seem to notice me, and I watched him for some time. He was dressed just as he had been before, and looked the same; but I could see him much more clearly than the first time, and if I had not known who it was, I should have thought it was a living man.

"I don't know how it was, but as I stood watching him I found that I wasn't afraid of him at all. He looked so sad and pitiful, and stood there so patiently, that I began to feel as I might toward some poor beggar; he seemed just like one, waiting for something to eat. Then I thought how he had pleaded the other day for assistance, and how I had turned him away—and although it was like death to face him again, I went into the hall and opened the door.

"The screen door was closed and locked, and we looked at each other through it. I could see every detail of the figure's face and dress as it stood there in the bright sunlight:—it was within three feet of me, and it was Deeming's without a shadow of a doubt.

"I don't know how long I stood there. I seemed to be in another world, and in a strange atmosphere which he may have brought with him. I had to make a strong effort, but finally succeeded in seeing and thinking clearly, and as he only looked appealingly at me and seemed not to be able to say anything, I was the first to speak.

"'I know who you are, this time,' I said. 'I told you never to come here again. Why have you done so?'

"'Madame,' he replied, 'I have come for help.'

"'I told you the other day I could do nothing for you,' I said.

"'But you can, if you will,' he answered, 'and there is nobody else I can reach. Don't be afraid of me—I won't hurt you. I need some one to show me Christian charity, and I thought you were kind and would help me.'"

"'Christian charity!'" I exclaimed, interrupting the recital for the first time: "was *that* what he said?"

"Those were his exact words," said my wife; "and it seemed almost blasphemy for such a creature to use them."

"They seem to me," I commented, "more like one of those stock phrases of which nearly every man has some, of one sort or another. Do you remember, in the letter Deeming wrote to you from the jail when you could not induce Miss Rounsfell to come to see him, how he said he was sorry you did not find her 'as Christianlike as yourself?' It may be a small point, but this appeal to your 'Christian charity' seems to confirm your belief that it was the apparition of Deeming that made it to you to-day. But what happened then?"

"Well," said she, taking up the thread of her

story, "while he was saying this he kept his eyes on mine—great, pleading eyes like those of a dog:—they made me think he was trying to say things for which he could not find words, and—I don't know why—I began to feel sorry for him.

" 'I don't understand at all what you mean,' I said. 'Your awful crimes horrify me, and I can hardly bear to look at you. Why should you distress me as you do?'

" 'I don't want to distress you,' he replied, 'but I must get out of this horrible place!'

" 'What do you mean by "this horrible place"? I cannot understand you.'

" 'I can't make you understand,' he said. 'They won't let me.' I don't know what he meant by 'they,' but I thought it was some beings that controlled him, though I could see nothing. Then he went on in a long, confused talk which I could only partly follow.

"The substance of what he said was this, as nearly as I could gather it. His body was buried in quicklime in a criminal's unmarked grave; I think he said under the wall of the jail, but of this I am not sure—and as long as a trace of it remained he was tied down to the scenes of his crime and punishment. If he could only find some one who would pity him, and show it by 'an act of Christian charity'—he used the expression again—his term of suffering here would be shortened, and he could 'go on;' that was the way he put it, although he did not seem to know what it meant. His talk was vague and rambling, and seemed to me very incoherent; but his distress was plain enough, and when he stopped speaking (which was not for some time, for he kept going back and repeating as if he were trying to make his meaning clearer) I had lost all feeling except that here was a creature in great trouble, and that I ought to help him if I could.

"When he had finished I asked him how I could show him the 'Christian charity' he had spoken about.

"'By giving me something,' he replied, 'and being sorry for me when you give it.'

"'I *am* sorry for you,' I said. 'Isn't that enough?'

"'No,' he answered, 'that isn't enough. You might have done it if you had bought the soap from me the other day.'

"'So it is money you want?' I asked.

"'Yes,' he said, 'money will do, or anything else that you value.'

"'Will you stay where you are until I can get

some?' I asked:—and he said, yes, he would stay where he was.

"So I went into my room and took some money from my purse, and went back and showed it to him; there was a half-crown, a shilling and some coppers—there they are, on the dressing table beside you."

"So you did not give them to him, after all?" I inquired, taking up the coins and examining them.

"Oh, yes, I did," replied my wife; "and that is the strangest part of the whole thing.

"As I said, I showed him the money and asked him if that would do; and he said it would.

"Then I said: 'I am not going to open this door. How can I give these coins to you?'

"'You don't need to open it,' he answered. 'There is a hat rack there behind you, with a marble shelf in it—put them on that shelf.'

"I stepped back to the hat rack and put the money on the shelf, watching him all the time. I glanced at the coins an instant as I laid them down, and when I looked at the door again there was nobody there. I instantly turned to the hat rack again, but the shelf was bare—the coins had disappeared, too!

"I rushed to the door to unlock it and run

into the street, for I thought Deeming had got into the house:—but just as I had my hand on the key I heard his voice in front of me.

" 'Don't be afraid,' the voice said. 'I haven't moved.'

" 'But how did you get the money?' I asked.

" 'You wouldn't understand if I should tell you,' replied the voice.

" 'But I can't see you!' I exclaimed.

" 'No,' said the voice, 'and you never will again. I have gone on.'

" 'But you are not going away with my money, are you?' I asked. 'Do you need it now?'

" 'No,' the voice replied, 'I do not need it. You gave it to me because you pitied me—I have no more use for it.'

" 'Can you give it back to me?' I asked.

" 'I *have* given it back,' said the voice. 'Look on the hat rack.'

"I heard something jingle behind me, and as I turned around I saw the coins all lying on the shelf again."

The conclusion of this prodigious history found me in a state very nearly approaching stupefaction. It was not so much the facts themselves which it embodied as the suggestions they inspired that appalled me, and the glimpse they seemed to afford of mysteries the human race has for ages shrinkingly guessed at, chilled me to the marrow of my bones. "Can such things be?" was the question I asked myself again and again as I struggled to regain my composure:—and although this experience seemed a natural and fitting sequence in the drama that had been enacted in that house under my own eyes, I am free to say I could not on the instant credit it.

My wife detected my hesitation at once, and said:

"I see you cannot believe what I have told you, and I do not wonder at it:—but it is true, for all that."

"I know you think so," I replied; "and in view of the very many other strange events you have taken part in—and I with you in a number of them—I ought to have no doubts. But this is the most staggering thing I ever heard of. Are you sure you were not dreaming?"

"Well," she said, with a laugh, "I am not in the habit of dreaming at eleven o'clock on a bright, sunny morning, and when I have the care of the house on my hands. And then, the dogs:—do you think *they* were dreaming, too?"

"Ah, yes!" I exclaimed; "what about the dogs?"

"I told you," she replied, "how they ran to the gate, barking, and then suddenly turned tail and rushed away in a panic as soon as they saw what was there. When Deeming had gone, I went out to look after them, but for a long time I could not find them. I called and I coaxed, but to no purpose. Finally I discovered them out in the farthest corner of the paddock, under the thick bushes, crowded together in a heap, and trembling as though they had been whipped. I had to crawl in and drag them out, but I couldn't induce them to come near the house; at last I had to carry them in, and all the afternoon they have stuck close to me as though they felt the need of protection. It is only half an hour ago that I got them into their kennels and chained them up. You had better go out and see them."

I did so, and found one kennel empty, and both dogs lying close together (as the length of their chains allowed them to do) in the straw of the other. I had never seen them do this before, since each was very jealous of intrusion by the other upon his quarters, and I was impressed by the circumstance. The poor brutes still showed unmistakable evidences of terror, whimpered and whined and licked my hand as I petted them, and set up a concerted and agonized howl of protest when I left them. There was no doubt whatever that they had been horribly frightened—if not by the ghost of Deeming, by what?—it was certainly no merely physical agitation that their actions showed.

CHAPTER XII

THE DEMONS OF THE DARK

TRUE to his promise, Deeming did not reappear, nor was there any subsequent manifestation that seemed referable to him. To what new plane he had "gone on," and whether to one higher or lower, we could only guess; the door that had closed upon his exit had evidently shut in forever (as had been our experience in certain other like cases) a mystery to which, for a moment, we had almost felt we were about to hold the key. Of the problem of the future life we had a hint of the terms of the solution, but the answer vanished before we could set it down below the ordered figures of the sum. Such, I believe, has been, is, and will be the constant fortune of all who venture far into the *penetralia* of the unseen. Now and then there seems to be an illumination—but it is not the radiance of discovered truth:—it is the lightning flash that warns away the profane intruder, and if defied it blasts him in body or in mind.

It was because of this conviction that my wife

THE HAUNTED BUNGALOW

and I, although having experience during many years of incomprehensible occurrences whose narration, should I set it down, would fill many books like this, steadfastly refrained from allowing ourselves to assume a mental attitude that might, so to speak, encourage them. Far from finding the influences (whatever they were—and on this point we were careful to make no inquiry, and never formulated any theory) reluctant to invitation to display themselves, we were at times compelled to offer strenuous opposition to their approach:—even a passive receptivity to strange phenomena was not free from peril, and our previous knowledge of the unbalancing of more than one inquiring mind that had pursued the subject of the occult with too great a temerity had convinced us that "that way danger lies"—and a very grave danger, too.

To that danger we ourselves, as I believe, finally came to be exposed in our life in the House on the Hill:—not because we were lured to seek out the origin and nature of the forces about us, and thus gave ourselves up to their influence, but because the more or less constant exercise of that influence could not fail to have that effect, in spite of ourselves:—and it is to show how, as it seemed, and why, this effect

—at first unsuspected—grew toward its sinister culmination, that I undertake the writing of this final chapter.

Meantime, I may say that the incidents attending the two spectral appearances that I have recorded, gave us occasion for much curious speculation, in which there was a certain relief in indulging ourselves. The garments from the wardrobe of the hangman; was the murderer doomed to go through all Eternity in this hideous attire? The offered sale of soap; is the occupation of "drummer" or "bagman" practiced beyond the Styx, and for what ghostly manufacturers are orders solicited? Was the soap a sample? Was it for the toilette or the laundry? What was its price per cake, and was there any discount by the box? Then the shade's appeal for "Christian charity," and the acceptance of it in the tangible form of coin of the realm! The money was returned again, but had it meanwhile been entered in some misty ledger to the credit of its temporary bearer? If deposits are made, and balance-sheets issued in the Dark World, then might Deeming's account seem to be heavily overdrawn. Dealing in phantom money, and liquidating of shadowy notes-of-hand!—do we carry with us into the Beyond not only our characters and personalities (as some believe) but also our occupations and ways of doing business? If Deeming's discarnated action was thus to be explained, he must have been in Hell, indeed!

Reflections such as these may strike the reader as flippant, but they were among the natural results of the circumstances. There was something so personal and intimate in these mid-day visits of the apparition, it was itself so seemingly tangible and even human, and in its expressions of thought and manifestations of emotion seemed to have experienced so slight an essential change from the conditions with which the living man had been acquainted, that there was little to excite horror in the event, after all. If the phantom had imparted to us no information, it had at least given us a hint that there was progress in the realms of the hereafter, and had awakened a vague belief that at the end of all there might be pardon. This suggestion was tenuous and elusive; but it was afforded, nevertheless, and I still cling to the hope that it inspired.

In writing this strange chronicle I have not attempted to set down all our experiences in that house of mystery, but only such as have seemed to me unusual, or representative of the manifestations as a whole. There were certain other phenomena so vague and evasive that I am unable to find words whereby to describe their nature or to convey the impression they caused:—all that I can say of them is that they seemed to invite us to an inquiry into some secret which the house contained, and to beckon to the success of such an investigation. We often discussed this apparent suggestion, but never acted upon it:—chiefly because, as I think, we were not at all sure it was not of subjective, rather than objective, origin—the natural result of the mental ferment which such a protracted series of weird happenings might be expected to cause. Moreover, as everything that had so far occurred had been without any conscious encouragement on our part, we felt some fear (as I have intimated above) of what might befall us if we endeavored to place ourselves completely *en rapport* with the agencies that seemed to be at work about us. Therefore we maintained as well as we could our isolated and non-conductive position, and refrained from all encouragement to the suggestions that were more and more forcibly borne in upon us that we should seek an understanding of the meaning of the things that had so much disturbed us.

Yet I cannot refrain from stating my conviction that the phenomena which I have endeavored to describe in these pages had their origin, not in any disturbed or morbid condition of the mind in any of the three persons who were affected by them, but in some undiscovered cause local and peculiar to the place of their occurrence. If this were not the case, it seems singular that manifestations of a like nature did not present themselves at other times and in other places. Any such persistent and startling incidents as those that were displayed in the House on the Hill were, happily, foreign elsewhere both to my wife's experience and to my own—such other influences as have seemed to come about us having apparently been unaffected by conditions of period and locality, and being almost always of a mild and gentle nature.

Whether our tacit refusal to seek a solution of the mystery that had so long brooded over us had anything to do with the even more serious and startling events that occurred during the final period of our residence, I cannot tell. I have often thought so:—at all events this record would be incomplete without setting them down.

It is not to be denied that the adventures in which we had participated for nearly a year, came finally to have a serious effect upon us, both physically and mentally. Our curiosity and interest had long ago become sated, and of late we had felt the slow but steady growth of something like apprehension:—an apprehension even more acute than that which might be inspired by any definite occasion for fear, since it looked forward to uncertainties for which there seemed to be no definition. But the days passed slowly by until only two weeks remained before the expiration of our lease, and, since the incident of the brooch which I have described, nothing seriously untoward had occurred.

Yet we had lately been conscious that the character of the influence that had so long possessed our habitation seemed to be undergoing a change. I cannot describe this change except to say that it took the form of an ominous quiescence. The elfish entities whose cantrips had served more to amuse and mystify than to annoy us, seemed suddenly to have abandoned the premises as if retiring before some superior approach, and the wraiths of the women and the child were no more seen or heard about the rooms or in the hall:—instead of these, we vaguely recognized the presence of a mighty force, which made itself manifest neither to the eye nor the ear, but was evident through some latent or inner sense whose function was to apprehend it. I cannot explain how the impression was conveyed, but we somehow knew that this presence was malignant and foreboded harm; and a disturbing uneasiness grew upon us rather than diminished as time elapsed, and everything remained upon the surface serene and calm.

While the familiar occurrences to which we had been accustomed never lost their sense of strangeness, the present cessation of them seemed more uncanny still; we had an uneasy and growing sense of something serious being about to happen, and often expressed to each other our common feeling of alarm. The circumstance that disquieted us most was that, whereas nearly all the events in which we had shared hitherto had taken place by day, this new obsession was felt chiefly at night:—it seemed to enwrap the house in an equal degree with the gathering darkness, and each evening at sundown we lighted every gas-jet, and sat or moved about together under the influence of an urgent craving for companionship. We were like spectators sitting in a theatre between two acts of a compelling performance; behind the lowered curtain a situation was preparing whose nature we could not guess; we apprehended rather than perceived that the stage was being reset, the scenery shifted, a new development provided for—and we feared beyond measure to see the curtain lift again, as we felt assured it would.

The climax came at last, and in a sudden and awful manner. Our nameless apprehension had caused us, of late, to spend as many evenings as possible abroad—visiting friends and acquaintances, or attending entertainments in the city. Returning late one night from the theatre, our friend and I went into the dining-room, while my wife retired to her chamber to prepare for bed. We had been chatting a few moments when we heard a piercing shriek from my wife's room; and rushing in we were horrified to see her standing close against the wall, her face white and drawn with terror, apparently striving to free herself from some being that held her firmly in its clutches. Her aspect was so unearthly that we stood for a moment literally frozen on the threshold:—then she seemed to be lifted up bodily and thrown across the bed, where she lay with eyes protruding, and hands frantically tearing at her throat as if trying to free herself from some powerful grip that was choking her. We rushed to her and raised her to a sitting position, but she was torn from us again and again, and from the gasping and throttled sounds that came from her throat we felt that she was dying. We cried out in incoherent frenzy to her unseen tormentors to be gone, and struck wildly at the air as if there were about her palpable objects of our blows. This dreadful struggle lasted for several minutes; at times we apparently prevailed, again we were overwhelmed:—finally the influence seemed to pass, and I laid her back upon the pillows, still panting and trembling but no longer suffocating, as she whispered: "Thank God, they have gone!"

This experience had been so frightful, and so foreign to all others that had befallen us, that I found myself reluctant to refer it to unnatural agencies, and tried to explain it as a fit of some kind by which my wife had been attacked—although I knew that she had never had such a seizure in all her life, and was in perfect physical and mental health. Moreover, when she soon complained of her throat hurting her, I looked more closely, and with amazement saw upon both sides of her neck the marks that no one could have mistaken as other than those left by the fingers of a pair of powerful hands!

At this sight the little courage that remained to me abandoned me entirely, and I could see that our friend was equally unmanned. "We must leave this house!" we exclaimed in the same breath:—and as we spoke my wife cried out: "Oh! they are here again!" and at once the ghastly combat was renewed.

This time our friend and I made no effort to fight against the demons—if such they were; we seized the half-conscious woman in our arms, and partly carried, partly dragged her out of the house. The Possession seemed to leave her at the door, and the fresh air soon revived her. But there was no going back for any of us that night. It was late summer, and the air was warm:—so, bareheaded, and with my wife guarded between her two male protectors, we walked the deserted streets until the rising of the sun gave us courage to return home.

I shall not forget those hours of midnight and early morning:—the serene and amethyst-colored Australian sky strewn with star-dust and set with twinkling constellations, and the dark earth about us—across which, as from time to time we approached the house from which we had been expelled, the light from its windows and from its open door gleamed balefully. All was silent within, but we feared the lurking presence and dared not enter, and after one or two returns remained only within view of it until daybreak was well advanced. Our conversation throughout the vigil need not be recorded, but the reader may guess its import:—the awful experience through which we had passed had brought powerfully to our minds the thought of Deeming in the feature of the throttling hands, since in all his murders there was evidence upon the throats of his victims that strangulation had preceded the operation of the knife. But my wife opposed this grisly suggestion:—it was not the shade of the murderer, she affirmed, that had attacked her, although she could give no description of her assailants—they were dark, formless shapes—resembling neither man nor beast; things more felt than seen, even to her.

Yet in spite of this assurance, when I re-entered the house and saw in its usual place above my writing table the plaster mould which I had carried from the murderer's cell in the Melbourne jail, I recalled with a new appreciation of their appositeness the words of the worthy governor.

Whatever the influence was that had appalled us, we had not sufficient courage to oppose it, and so hastened our preparations for departure that we finally quitted the house a week before our lease expired; and within a month saw the shores of Australia fade behind us as our steamer turned its prow toward Aden, Suez, and Marseilles. There was one recurrence of the phenomenon I have just described during the last few nights of our possession, but we evaded it by taking to the street again, and again passing the night therein.

It was on a sunny morning in early March—the month answering in the inverted seasons of the Antipodes to September of northern latitudes—that we turned the key that locked us out for the last time from that house of shadows. As we reached the street we turned with one accord to look back upon it:—how inviting it appeared in the brilliant sunshine, amid its attractive surroundings of grassy lawn set with shrubs in flower, its smiling orchard and garden! We looked into one another's faces, and each saw therein the reflection of his own thoughts:—there was the relief such as they feel who awake from an oppressive dream; yet the place had been our home!

THE END